THE
LIFE OF
Mohawk JOSEPH
BRANT

Mohawk ☀ THE LIFE OF JOSEPH BRANT

by John Jakes

Illustrations by Roger Hane

Crowell-Collier Press
Collier-Macmillan Limited, London

This is for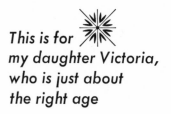
my daughter Victoria,
who is just about
the right age

Library of Congress Catalog Card Number: 76–75898

The Macmillan Company
Collier-Macmillan Canada Ltd., Toronto, Ontario
Printed in the United States of America
FIRST PRINTING

Preface

This book tells the life story of one of the most unusual Indian chiefs who ever lived. In the opinion of many historians, Joseph Brant is the only true statesman the American Indian tribes have ever produced.

The book covers Brant's entire life, but deals mainly with his youth and his career during the Revolutionary War. The war was the high point in Brant's effort to save his people by means of an idea—a great and powerful Indian league.

Brant himself was a mixture of many traits. He combined the fierceness of the woodland Indian with the good manners of an English nobleman's son. His whole life was a process of growth, as he was changed from a savage to a highly civilized man.

He was a brave warrior. Yet religious training helped him to be merciful in battle.

He longed to mingle on equal terms with white men, and sometimes even imagined himself a true citizen of the British Empire. But he never really turned his back on his people or allowed himself to forget his Indian heritage.

Now that the American Revolution is well into history, it is possible to look at Brant's career with more sympathy than did the colonists who won their freedom from England. Because he fought with the British, Brant is not generally considered one of our American heroes.

But he can be judged—fairly—as a remarkable enemy, and a great man.

Contents

one A Mohawk Boyhood
1742–1754

The boy's Mohawk name was Thayendanegea. It meant Two-Sticks-of-Wood-Bound-Together. It also meant Strength.

He was born in 1742 and raised in the wilderness along the upper Ohio River, far from the homeland of his mother in the Mohawk Valley of what is now New York State. He might have lived and died Thayendanegea, unknown by any other name, except for the presence on the American continent of an unusual Englishman.

Sir William Johnson had come to the colonies in 1738 to manage a tract of land owned by a relative. Born in Ireland, Johnson was a tall, robust, vigorous man of education and charm. Soon he had land of his own, and was trading actively with the Indians.

The Indians did not trust many white traders. But they found Johnson to be honest and—surprisingly—interested in learning all he could about Indian life. He was adopted by the Mohawk and learned their language thoroughly. The Indians christened him Warrahiyagey—He-Who-Does-Much.

Johnson began his career in the colonies as a sort of unofficial representative of the British king among the Indians. Before long, however, his close kinship with the tribes was given official status. Governor George Clinton of New York appointed him superintendent of Iroquois affairs in 1744, a time when the British were becoming more and more concerned about maintaining Indian friendship.

The British knew that the support of the Indian tribes would be important in case of a serious war with France. French traders were thick in America when Johnson arrived. They had explored widely, established forts, and controlled much of the fur trade from their outposts in Canada.

Trouble looked certain; the prize was too big for trouble to be avoided. The prize was nothing less than control of the eastern half of America and the southern part of Canada and all the new land and the vast supply of fur that went with it.

When Johnson came to the colonies, the most important Indians were the members of the Iroquois nation. The Iroquois lived mainly in New York. Actually, they were not a single tribe, but five tribes sharing a basic language.

The Seneca lived in the area just south of present-day Rochester. The Cayuga were found along the shore of the lake of the same name. The Onondaga were centered near the modern city of Syracuse. The Oneida dwelled along Oneida Lake. And the Mohawk inhabited the beautiful Mohawk River Valley.

Originally called the Five Nations, the tribes eventually admitted a sixth to membership. The Tuscarora Indians had come to New York from Virginia. With their addition, the loose union of related tribes became known as the Six Nations of the Iroquois.

Johnson's job as superintendent was to promote and strengthen the loyalty of the Iroquois. He was very good at the job. He roved the frontier, spreading his message of English good will. Soon many of the people of the Six Nations came to think of him as almost a god. Certainly he was their friend.

On one of his trips, Johnson may well have met Thayendanegea's mother at Canajoharie, a prosperous Mohawk settlement. For years after the boy Thayendanegea was born, it was often said that he was Sir William's son. It is quite possible. Johnson did have a number of children whose mothers were Indian women.

But there is no definite evidence, except Johnson's great interest in the boy's welfare at a later time. It is just as possible that Thayendanegea's father was the full-blooded Mohawk chief of the Wolf tribe, Nichaus or Nickus Brant.

Like most Indians, Chief Brant had more than one name. His given Indian name was Tehowagh-wengaraghkwin. His English name had been passed down from his father—Thayendanegea's grand-father—who was called King of the Mohawks, or King Brant.

The name Brant is thought to have come from a family of English settlers with whom these Mohawk chiefs associated. This family's name was Barnet.

It was not unusual for colonists to give special English names to Indians with whom they came in contact. Nor was it unusual for the Indians to adopt these names.

But Thayendanegea's parentage is made even more cloudy because his mother did not actually marry Nichaus Brant until after the boy's birth in 1742. Indeed, she was married to another Mohawk at the time she left the neat, well-settled village of Canajoharie with its barns, fields, and fruit trees, and set out cross-country for the much wilder hunting lands along the Ohio River.

Why she went is still another mystery.

The Iroquois often went to the Ohio to hunt wild game and escape the sight of settlers. Already many white men were moving into upstate New York. Perhaps the boy's mother accompanied such a band of restless Mohawks. In any case, Thayendanegea was born in the woods of the Ohio in 1742, and spent his early years there.

Freedom was highly prized by the Iroquois. Personal freedom was one of the great experiences of an Indian boy growing up in the forests of the western frontier. The young Thayendanegea soon learned that he was free to do whatever he wished. In fact, he was expected to live in this manner.

He was free to hunt. He was free to paddle a canoe, free to play games, free to sleep whenever he was tired, free to eat as much as he wished any time.

No adult scolded the young Mohawk boy if he grew moody or cross or lost his temper completely. This, too, was accepted as the Indian way. A raging temper indicated the approach of manhood. Later in life, when Thayendanegea was fighting to hold back some of his hot-tempered Indian brothers, he would have cause to regret the early emphasis on doing anything one wished, at any cost. But at the time, growing up along the Ohio, it seemed the most natural thing in the world.

The strong belief in freedom that filled the mind of the young Mohawk boy is not so hard to understand. All around him he saw a land of great beauty. No one lived there except his people. The land seemed to have been created for his personal use and enjoyment. What was wrong with that?

Nothing—until the British and the French began to settle the continent, bringing with them odd notions about law, God, ownership of land, and their right to rule because they were more powerful.

The area where the Mohawk boy grew up was, by and large, both isolated and peaceful. The Iroquois kept all other tribes out. The mountains of Pennsylvania kept the settlers penned up along the coast.

But another kind of white man did reach the upper Ohio. Very possibly the first one that Thayendanegea saw was a trader.

The traders who came to the outlying villages carried packs loaded with strange and fabulous articles. There were glittering beads and dazzling bits of costume jewelry, stout hatchets and keen knives. There were cooking pots and shiny ovals of silver in which a boy could see his own face. There were guns for the men, sewing items for the women, and a fiery drink called rum. The trader passed it around to the braves as a symbol of his friendship.

These traders were strange, fantastic figures with their pale skins, their coarse clothing, and their seemingly endless supply of trinkets and weapons. The boy Thayendanegea could not help but have been impressed. And he must have realized that all this glittering wealth came from somewhere. The white men, then, lived differently from his own people.

Perhaps he was a little frightened of what he saw. But everything points to the fact that he must have been very much interested, too. He wanted to explore this fascinating and unusual world peopled by the white-skins!

He soon got the chance.

The boy had an older half-sister, Molly. Sometime around 1752, she went to visit her former home in the Mohawk Valley. She was a "very spritely and beautiful Indian girl of about sixteen" when she caught Sir William Johnson's eye.

According to one story, Molly and some other Indians were watching a colorful review put on by British soldiers. One officer rode by on a spirited horse. Molly asked if she could jump up and ride behind him. Laughing, the officer said of course.

He probably didn't think she could do it without help.

Molly surprised him. With one agile leap she was on the horse. Her arms circled the officer's waist and her dark hair streamed behind her as the horse raced off. There was applause as the horse swiftly circled the parade ground. Sir William was in the crowd. He noticed the pretty Indian girl, and immediately took a fancy to her.

Johnson lived in a big stone house by the Mohawk River. He invited Molly to come and live there as his housekeeper, and take care of three of his white children, Nancy, Polly, and John. Molly was soon accepted as far more than a housekeeper, though. Johnson began treating her like a wife.

Soon she took complete charge of the household kitchens. She took to sitting at Sir William's dinner table when he entertained guests. People began calling her "the Lady Johnson."

Meanwhile, faraway events were shaping Thayendanegea's life, too.

By 1754, colonists in Virginia, including members of the distinguished Washington family, had been granted land in the upper Ohio Valley. The King urged the Ohio Company of Virginia to build a fort at the fork where the Monongahela and Allegheny rivers joined to form the Ohio. It was understood that the Virginians would use soldiers in case the French tried to stop them.

In the spring of '54, French troops surprised the

little band of colonists busy constructing their fort, which they called Necessity. A relief column was already on the way. Among its officers was Lieutenant Colonel George Washington of Virginia.

When the French attacked the column, Washington's commander was killed. He took over and marched the troops into Fort Necessity. The French attacked again. Washington was forced to surrender. It was clear that a last, great war between England and France for control of the North American continent was in the making.

At first the king of England, George II, was reluctant to have any part of it. "Let Americans fight Americans," was his comment. But the King's ministers led him to change his mind. George sent two of his best generals to the colonies to take charge of the coming war.

As a result of these developments, Sir William Johnson's standing rose. As superintendent of Iroquois affairs, he was already considered by the Indians to be the greatest of all living Englishmen. But now his own government gave him more duties. He was made a baronet and put in command of military units. His home in the Mohawk Valley, originally called Mount Johnson, was heavily fortified and renamed Fort Johnson.

The house quickly became a center of colonial affairs. Soldiers and Negro slaves guarded it. Indian chiefs and British governors and army officers visited it on a regular basis. There was much talk of

war. Just about this same time, Molly arranged to have Sir William notice her half-brother.

Thayendanegea was a bright, quick lad. He seemed eager to learn the ways of the great world outside the Mohawk villages to which he had traveled with his mother. Finally Molly's efforts were rewarded. The boy was summoned to Fort Johnson and invited to live there.

He would be a full member of the family, Johnson said. He would share the table with Johnson's own white children. Was he interested? It was a dazzling opportunity for a twelve-year-old. Perhaps a little frightening, too. But the boy quickly accepted.

Johnson kept his word. He was kind to Thayendanegea. But the boy soon sensed a difference in the way the white visitors to the house treated Indians as opposed to white men.

Indians were inferior. This belief was sometimes spoken aloud. More often, it was expressed in a laugh or a glance. It angered the boy. Apart from Johnson, no white man was worthy to stand in the shadow of an Iroquois!

The boy yearned to prove that the white men were wrong. He wanted to show them that he could be as clever and polite as they were. He wanted to prove that he could be as skillful in warfare, as cunning in matters of government, as any Englishman. To do that, he realized, he would have to learn all he could about the world in which the white man lived.

In Johnson's house he could begin to do just that. He was surrounded by white people. He studied them—and their everyday objects and clothing. China dishes, silverware. Chairs, oil paintings. Ribbons, skirts, suits of fine cloth, leather boots.

The change from a wilderness boy to a more civilized one was helped along by one other circumstance. Johnson had given him another name. Almost everyone called him by it. Thayendanegea was now known as Joseph Brant.

The boy made up his mind. He would succeed in this strange new world! But not as Thayendanegea.

As Joseph Brant.

two

The First Warpath
1755–1761

There were many things for Brant to learn in the great house that overlooked the Mohawk River. Chief among them was English.

Both Johnson and Molly encouraged the boy to learn the language. Brant didn't have much trouble doing it. Like all boys of his tribe, he had been trained to imitate sounds. Indians used the calls of birds or the cries of animals to communicate with each other in the forest. This ability helped Brant pronounce, then understand, English words quickly. He was spurred on by Johnson's promise that if he knew the white man's tongue, he would be used as an interpreter. He could then go along with Johnson on military expeditions.

This Brant wanted to do very much. He and Johnson had formed a strong son-father relationship. This fact is often pointed out to support the claim that Brant was actually Sir William's child.

In any case, the household on the Mohawk had its civilizing influence. Brant learned when to say "please" and "thank you" and, perhaps unhappily, he also learned that a white boy didn't always get his way. Sir William's people lived differently from the free, do-as-you-please Iroquois. Yet Brant did not rebel. He actually took to the new way of life with enthusiasm.

During his first year at the Johnson house, Brant formed a strong friendship with a boy called William of Canajoharie. William was one of Johnson's many children by Indian women. He was younger than Brant, but bigger and stronger. The boys played Indian games together. One of their favorite pastimes was wrestling.

Because he was larger, William usually won. Brant's strong will at this early age is shown by the fact that he never really gave in to William, even though he was beaten time after time. After every defeat, Brant was up quickly and pleading for one more chance, one more bout.

The rivalry became so well known in the neighborhood that the boys often put on wrestling matches at public gatherings. Brant wanted to beat William in the worst way, especially with an audience of white people watching. He couldn't help feeling that, as a Mohawk, he was looked down on by the white-skins with whom he lived. He wanted to show them just how good he was.

History doesn't reveal whether Brant ever bested his friend and opponent. But his courage and his refusal to run away from a challenge were soon well known around the Johnson home. Sir William approved.

The struggle between the British and French,

meantime, was growing hotter. And things were not going well for the British.

One of the two senior officers whom the King had sent to the colonies was General Edward Braddock. In July of 1755, a force of British regulars and colonials under his command was ambushed by the French and Indians near Fort Duquesne and was defeated. Braddock was fatally wounded. The retreat was led by the commander of the colonials, Lieutenant Colonel Washington. It was a stinging setback to the King's cause.

Early the next year, Johnson announced that he planned to march north from Albany toward the French post at Crown Point on Lake Champlain. He would command a force of about 3,500 colonial soldiers—called "Bostonians" by the Indians—and an auxiliary of about 400 red men, including some from each of the Six Nations—Mohawk and Oneida, Onondaga and Cayuga, Seneca and Tuscarora. Joseph Brant wanted to go with the war party.

Before the expedition got under way, a war council was held at Fort Johnson. Members of the Six Nations had been summoned by means of a big belt of purple and white wampum, which was carried from village to village. Brant watched with mounting excitement as the leaders of the tribes arrived. The most powerful was the old but still-ferocious war chief of the Nations, King Hendrick. He was of Brant's tribe. By tradition, a war chief of the Nations always came from the Mohawks.

A total of around 1,200 Indians showed up for the three-day meeting. They gathered in a meadow that sloped down to the river and listened closely while each important chief made a speech. Most of the speeches urged the Indians to support the King in the war.

Finally Johnson rose to make his own speech. It was a loud, angry oration. The French were massing in the north. Soon they would rush down and destroy both the English and the Indian settlements. Unless they could be stopped, the Six Nations might well find themselves in wild retreat to the ocean, driven out of their homelands!

A frenzy of yelling and rumble of tom-toms greeted the speech. The noise increased when Johnson reminded them that he was a true friend of the Indians. Didn't he know their language? Wasn't he speaking to them in their own tongue right now? The Indians shouted approval.

Challenging them to make war, Johnson raised the wampum belt and threw it on the ground.

One of the chiefs rushed forward with a yell. He seized the belt and thrust it up over his head. It was a sign that the challenge had been accepted. The yelling and the thunder of drums broke out anew.

Brant found it thrilling. He had to convince Johnson that he should be allowed to go on the expedition even though he was only thirteen years old.

Brant spoke to Molly. At first she didn't like the

idea. Then, when she saw that he was determined, she promised to speak to Johnson.

Johnson called the boy to him. After warning Brant that he would be expected to fight as fiercely as any full-grown warrior, he agreed to let Brant come along. It was a moment of triumph for the young Mohawk.

Brant's first taste of battle came on September 8, 1756, at Lake George. There Johnson's party met a force of about 1,400 French and Indians under the command of a Baron Dieskau.

Johnson and his army camped on the shore of the lake. Early in the morning, a colonel rushed in to report that a wagon train of supplies coming up from the south had been ambushed by the French. Johnson immediately decided to send five hundred men south to engage the enemy troops. Coming from the north, the French had apparently circled around the English camp in the night.

Johnson ordered King Hendrick to take his Indians and go with the five hundred colonials. Meantime another five hundred men would be sent north to attack Crown Point.

King Hendrick didn't believe that five hundred soldiers were enough. By way of example, he picked up a single stick and broke it. Then he put together a bundle. He showed that these sticks could not be easily broken.

Brant stood with the older warriors, listening closely. He looked like an Indian on the warpath now. He wore only a breechcloth. His face was painted, and all his hair was cut off except for a scalp lock that was dressed with bear grease.

Hendrick went on to give a little sermon. The Six Nations were like that bundle of sticks, he said. United, they were very strong. Divided, they could be easily destroyed.

Johnson finally agreed to send a thousand men south with the Indians. The party set off.

Brant carried a musket as well as a scalp knife. The party moved cautiously ahead into a gorge. Suddenly muskets exploded from an ambush in a thicket.

Retreat was impossible because the gorge was

packed with men. Hendrick was shot off his horse by the first attack. He fell dead as white-uniformed French soldiers and their Canadian Indian allies appeared from the thicket.

The battle was on. Brant was in the middle of it, shooting his musket and thrusting with his knife in vicious hand-to-hand combat.

As the battle raged, reinforcements arrived from Johnson's camp. Under the covering fire of these reinforcements, what was left of the English force was able to retreat.

Johnson hadn't been idle at the camp. He had built barricades of felled trees. Brant and the others got into position behind the barricades and directed a withering fire at the pursuing French. Cannon boomed from the barricades, too, and soon Johnson called the order for the English and Indians to move out and destroy the attackers.

Howling, Iroquois and Bostonians leaped over the great tree trunks and charged. In moments the French were running, scattering. . . .

When the battle was over, Brant realized he had passed his first test. He had fought well. Perhaps he had killed several Frenchmen. He couldn't be sure because of the confusion. But he had gained experience on the battlefield. He was proud of that.

An incident at the end of the day left another vivid impression on him.

One of the French prisoners brought into the camp was the commander of the enemy force, Baron

Dieskau himself. The Iroquois screamed and howled for the Baron's instant death. After all, hadn't the French killed the Mohawk leader King Hendrick?

Sir William refused their frenzied pleas. The Indians then said they wanted to torture the Frenchman. Again Johnson refused.

Brant wondered who was right. His Indian blood told him that the Baron should be punished. On the other hand, the Indians certainly had taken revenge for the ambush. They were carrying many fresh scalps.

The boy finally decided that Johnson was correct in showing mercy to the French commander. What would be gained by slaughtering him? This early example of mercy to captives helped set a pattern in Brant's later life.

Brant returned from the battle in the north feeling grown up and fully worthy of wearing the badge of honor of a Mohawk warrior—a single eagle feather in his headdress. One account reports that Brant even brought back two battlefield souvenirs— a pair of white trousers that had belonged to a French soldier, and a scalp.

Johnson's standing rose again as a result of the Lake George victory. It was the first and only major land battle that the British had been able to win during five years of the French and Indian War. Brant knew he had been right in deciding months ago that Johnson was a great man.

In 1758, at age sixteen, Brant again took to the

warpath. He was one of the Mohawk guides who led Colonel John Bradstreet's soldiers north to Fort Frontenac, on the northern shore of Lake Ontario.

During the campaign against this fort, many of the regulars and colonials were stricken with fever. At first Brant was inclined to jeer at the physical weakness of the soldiers. But the attack was a success. The fort fell on August 27. Brant returned home with more respect for white men. In spite of widespread illness, they had fought hard, and won. A Mohawk could admire this kind of courage. It was his own kind.

The year 1759 turned the tide. In England, Secretary of State William Pitt the Elder was directing the colonial war along new, more vigorous lines. He had committed the King to a policy of spending whatever was necessary to bring about a total victory. Reinforcements poured into the colonies, and by 1759, the time for a new and hopefully final series of attacks on the French strongholds had come.

One English army moved up the St. Lawrence River to strike Quebec. Another swept toward the French forts at Ticonderoga and Crown Point, intending to take them and march on to Canada to join the first. A third army, two thousand soldiers commanded by General John Prideaux, was to make a long march down the shore of Lake Ontario from Oswego to Fort Niagara, an important

French post located where the Niagara River poured into the lake.

With Prideaux went nine hundred warriors of the Six Nations, all recruited by Johnson. Brant, now seventeen, was a member of the Indian company.

The army bombarded the fort with cannon and mortars. But the French defenders returned fire and stubbornly refused to give up. A mortar blast at the start of the siege killed General Prideaux. Johnson took over.

A scout brought word that a French relief column was approaching along the river from the direction of Niagara Falls. Johnson sent 150 regulars and all of his Indians up river to prepare a breastwork and halt the column's passage.

Months earlier, a number of Onondagas had deserted to the French, and with the outcome of the Fort Niagara battle now in doubt, some of Johnson's Indians showed signs of wanting to do the same. Loyal to Johnson, Brant urged them to stand fast. Because he was Johnson's pupil, the Indians listened to him. They held their positions as the French advanced.

A stiff fight took place along the edge of the Niagara gorge. The French eventually broke and ran. Brant and his companions pursued them for some distance, taking many scalps. The lesson of mercy learned at Lake George was temporarily forgotten.

By sunset on July 25, 1759, the Union Jack flew over Fort Niagara. The British controlled the Great Lakes at last.

In September, the army of Brigadier General Wolfe met that of the Marquis de Montcalm on the plains of Abraham at Quebec. Quebec fell. The war for domination of the North American continent was all but over. Britain had won.

As the war ground to its end, Johnson returned to his home in the Mohawk Valley. Brant went with him. Now Johnson had time to devote to family affairs. One item of importance was the future of his young Mohawk protégé.

Brant had proved his skill in battle. He had also shown leadership ability. Now Johnson had a real chance to affect forever the direction of Brant's life—to make him a lifelong friend of the British. Brant could be much more than just another chief, Johnson sensed. But he had to be trained.

In 1761 it was decided that Joseph Brant, age nineteen, should start school.

three

Test of Loyalty
1761–1763

Eleazer Wheelock had studied religion as a student at Yale. In 1735, he became the pastor of a small Congregational church at Lebanon, Connecticut. Finding that the young men of the area were poorly prepared to do college work, he started a school in his home. One of his early students was a young Mohican Indian.

The boy's intelligence and rapid progress changed many of Wheelock's ideas about the learning abilities of the Indians. He decided to establish a free school where both white and Indian boys could be educated. He did so in 1754.

By 1761 Wheelock's free school was well known. It was natural that Johnson would pick the school as the place where Joseph Brant would gain his much-needed formal education. Brant traveled to Connecticut.

Because of a lack of money, the Lebanon school ultimately failed. Wheelock was invited to go north to New Hampshire, where a new college called Dartmouth was being started. Because of his experience in teaching young men, Wheelock was chosen as its first president. He would look back on his years at Lebanon with some unhappiness. He had tried to do the Christian thing in educating young Indians. But he had not been very successful—except in the case of Brant.

From time to time the school had as many as two dozen young Iroquois students. None, however, seemed to take to lessons the way Brant did. He quickly learned to read and write English from primers and hornbooks. He worked hard, in contrast to the other boys. Their behavior made it clear that they would much rather be back in their villages doing exactly as they wished.

At Lebanon Brant attended the regular chapel services that Schoolmaster Wheelock held for students. Brant began to learn why certain white men frowned on killing.

The reasons were written in a book from which Wheelock read aloud. The Holy Bible was familiar to Brant by name. Most of its contents were not. He was particularly fascinated by the Old Testament story of Joseph, the slave of the pharoah of Egypt, whose wisdom saved the land from famine.

Perhaps Brant saw himself as a modern Joseph serving the modern pharoah—the British king—in order to make life easier for his own people.

Brant did so well at the school that he soon became a welcome guest at the homes of some of the teachers Wheelock employed. Two of the men Brant met in this way had a great influence on his life.

The first was Samuel Kirkland, a missionary who

would later preach and teach among the Oneidas.

At first Brant was simply Kirkland's pupil in Bible study. But Kirkland soon realized that the boy could help him prepare for his own work among the Indians. Brant took turns being the teacher, helping Kirkland learn Iroquois.

He also caught some of Kirkland's strong religious feeling. Perhaps the way of the Bible represented the true way; perhaps by becoming Christians, and being merciful instead of bloodthirsty, his people could live as brothers with the white men, and find peace.

As Brant learned more about the New and Old Testaments, Kirkland suggested that he tackle the task of translating parts of the Bible into the Iroquois language. There was presently no way in which the Indians could read the word of God. The idea stayed with Brant for many years, and finally bore fruit.

The second man who influenced Brant was Charles Jeffrey Smith, another teacher at the school. He was Brant's personal tutor, and he was filled with a desire much like Kirkland's. One day he planned to leave the quiet classroom and work among the Indians as a missionary.

As Brant's second year at the school came to a close, Smith had an idea. During the summer he wanted to make a tour of the Iroquois towns to see conditions first hand. Who would be a better guide and interpreter than Brant?

Early in 1763 Smith wrote Johnson, asking for his permission to let Brant go with him. The letter praised the boy's ability:

". . . He is a promising Youth, of a sprightly Genius, singular Modesty, and a Serious Turn. . . . I know of none so well calculated to answer my End as He is—in which design he would very Willingly and cheerfully engage should Your Honour consent to and approve of it. He has so much endeared Himself to me by his Amiable Deportment, his Laudable Thirst after and Progress in Learning, that did I not apprehend this would be as beneficial to Him, as advantageous to me, I should neither desire his Assistance nor solicit your Approbation. . . ."

Wheelock too had plans for Brant. Before the youth left for the wilderness with Smith, the schoolmaster wanted to take him on a trip of various coastal cities. He wanted to show Brant the ways of the white world. Obviously, Wheelock felt that Brant was fast abandoning his old, tribal ties and becoming more and more civilized every day. He wanted to help the process along.

Brant was even turning out to look more civilized than most Indians.

Like most Mohawks he was tall, muscular, and carried himself proudly. But unlike a Mohawk, his face was not particularly angular or savage-looking. In fact, the surviving pictures of Brant show a rounded, almost gentle face. In addition, his skin was paler than that of his fellow Indians. This only convinced those he met that he really was Johnson's son.

But events were taking place on the western frontier that would completely disrupt Brant's schooling, and again turn his life onto a different course. In the West of 1763, a chief was talking war.

The chief was Pontiac, powerful leader of the Ottawa.

Pontiac had had a long and bloody career as a warrior. He had fought beside the French against the English. When the French forts in the West were occupied by soldiers of the Crown, Pontiac agreed not to attack, provided the Indians were treated well and their rights respected. Pontiac demanded unlimited free ammunition. The British had no intention of arming the Indians in this way. Pontiac realized what Joseph Brant would realize, too. For all their polite words, the colonists really had just one goal. They wanted to take away the land and the power of the Indians. In that way they would make their own settlements secure.

Encouraged by a few French agents still lingering near the western Great Lakes, Pontiac traveled among the towns of the Ottawa, Pottawattomi, and Ojibwa tribes. He got promises that the tribes would go on the warpath. Then he made his plans.

On signal, each tribe would attack the nearest British fort. Pontiac himself planned to destroy Detroit. At the last minute his scheme was discovered, and he was forced to put the fort under siege.

By the end of May, 1763, the "Conspiracy of Pontiac" was in full flame.

Fort Sandusky fell. Then Fort Miami and Fort Venango and Fort Presque Isle—all the British forts west of Niagara, in fact, except for heavily defended Fort Pitt and Fort Detroit. The latter continued to resist Pontiac's personally led siege.

In the East, the Six Nations were stirring. Pontiac's messengers came with wampum belts, recruiting more warriors.

Until it broke into the open, the rebellion in the West was a well-kept secret. But the Lady Johnson—Molly—had close ties with the Indian communities. She soon heard rumors about some of the Iroquois wanting to march west to make war. She sent Joseph Brant a letter at the Lebanon school. Written in Iroquois, the letter ordered the young man to return home immediately.

Molly understood her brother's potential ability as a leader.

She felt that the new war was extremely serious—too serious for him to waste his time on education.

Eleazer Wheelock pleaded with Brant to stay. It was a kind of contest between the teacher's religious beliefs and the call of Brant's Indian heritage. This call urged him to be in the center of the storm.

As for Johnson, getting ready to move into a new and even bigger home on the Mohawk River—Johnson Hall—the outbreak was a serious storm indeed.

As recently as April, things had seemed calm.

Johnson had been in perfect command of his Indian allies throughout the region. And so he was stunned by the sudden violence. Then, as Pontiac went to Detroit and British forts burned, the next blow fell. The loyalty of the Iroquois seemed to fade away.

The Seneca, largest and most warlike of the tribes of the Six Nations, went over to Pontiac's side at once. Seneca braves rushed west. The Onondaga and Cayuga showed signs of doing the same. There was talk of the Mohawk deserting, planning to turn on their British friends, loot, burn, spread the rebellion into the East.

It was in this tense situation that Brant found himself when he decided to go home.

But what should he do? Traditional loyalty said he should support his own people.

But support them against Johnson? Sir William's prestige sagged badly the minute his allies began to desert. Not standing up for Johnson was unthinkable. The man was like his father. And didn't the teachings of Jesus say that killing was wrong?

Besides, traditional Iroquois policy said that the Six Nations could only live safely by remaining friends with the white men who controlled the East Coast. With British allies supplying them with guns, ammunition, and other necessities, the Iroquois were free to focus their attention on their western borders, protecting them from anyone who threatened, be he Frenchman or rival Indian. Thus it had always been. Thus it should be now.

Even so, Brant wondered whether Pontiac might be partly right.

Brant heard Pontiac's message from his fellow Mohawk. Pontiac said that the white men had to be driven away before they swallowed every last piece of Indian land. The great war chief swore that no Indian would ever receive fair treatment from a foreign master—and especially not from a British one.

This Brant doubted. He knew and trusted Johnson. And yet one part of Pontiac's argument made sense.

Pontiac preached Indian unity. It reminded Brant of the meaning of the weak single stick versus the strong bundle. If indeed the Indians were to be pushed from their land, they had to stand together to resist. Pontiac had already united the western tribes to destroy the colonial outposts. Was he wrong?

Finally Brant decided he was. Brant's loyalty to Johnson won out.

So, in the frantic summer of 1763, Brant traveled through the towns of the eastern Iroquois in a desperate effort to keep them from taking the warpath.

He was twenty-one years old now, fully matured. He was a fluent and persuasive speaker. He visited the Oneida and the Mohawk, counseling with chiefs, pleading, arguing. He won grudging promises that the two tribes would not desert their friend Johnson.

Brant was a bit surprised at the reception he got in the towns. Some Indians had mocked him when he went away to school. Now chiefs much older than he listened carefully to every word he said. Perhaps it was his close association with Sir William. Perhaps it was because he had proved his ability as a fighter, and could not be accused of being a coward. Perhaps it was because of his obvious intelligence and sincerity. In any event, when he kept the Oneidas and Mohawks off the warpath, the situation in upper New York became much less tense.

In early August, the Indians suffered a serious defeat near Fort Pitt. Furthermore, Pontiac was having no luck with the siege of Fort Detroit. Finally, in November, he was forced to stop the siege and creep away. His six-month rebellion was almost a complete failure.

In the East, however, a few Indians kept talking of war. As winter approached, Johnson decided that he had to crush this disloyalty. He sent out a volunteer force of loyal Mohawk and Oneida under the command of one of his aides, Andrew Montour. Brant went along.

Montour's Indians descended on at least four villages on the upper Susquehanna River and burned them one by one. All the winter stores of corn were destroyed. Those braves who had spoken most loudly in support of Pontiac were taken prisoner.

The news traveled like a shockwave through the eastern frontier. Iroquois had attacked their own people, in support of the white men! Those who thought about continuing to fight with Pontiac now thought twice. The rebellion in the East was over before it really ever started.

As the winter of 1764 wore on, the rebellion faded to a memory. It was something to be haggled about in the endless peace negotiations in which Johnson became engaged. Brant may have felt guilty about his role in attacking people of his own blood and burning their towns. But he had made what he thought was the right decision.

Actually, it proved to have been the wrong one.

Later, when Brant himself would try to unite the tribes against the very enemy Pontiac had fought, too many chiefs of the Six Nations would remember the rebellion. Too many would remember that Brant had attacked Iroquois villages on behalf of his friends the English.

Could it be that at Wheelock's school Brant had betrayed his heritage, and become more white than Mohawk? He often wondered about it.

Joseph Brant, age twenty-two, was approaching the time in his life when he would feel his closest kinship with the white men. This peaceful period would last just ten years.

At the start of it he took a wife, Christine. She was the daughter of a chief of the Oneida. She was also a convert to the Christian religion, and often preached Christianity to her people in her native tongue. Probably this was one of the reasons Brant was attracted to her.

The newly married couple settled at Canajoharie. Brant bought a farm of one hundred acres, and built a frame house for himself and his wife. The house was full of all of the standard items found in the home of any white frontier family: furniture, dishes, a stone fireplace, a cellar for storing food through the winter.

Brant farmed fields, raised livestock. The marriage was evidently a happy one. Christine bore him two children: a son, Isaac, who was to be a serious problem in years to come, and a daughter, Christiana, whom Brant idolized.

Though Brant was busy with activities more suited to a white man than to an Indian—he even wore broadcloth suits to receive guests—he did not forget his people. Their problems grew worse by the day.

More and more settlers were arriving in the Mohawk Valley. The demand for farmland increased. Most of the acreage around the most important Mohawk villages—"castles," the Mohawk called them—was rapidly being stripped of game and converted to farmland. Thus the Indians were faced with a hard choice: either turn to farming themselves, or sell the bits of land which they still owned and move west, hoping to find better hunting ground.

Unlike Brant, most of the Indians had no interest in raising crops. So the frenzy to sell land became intense.

Before long the Mohawk's "castle" at Fort Hunter, was surrounded on all sides by land owned by settlers. Canajoharie was rapidly being encircled in the same way. And both the Indians who wanted to sell, and those who refused, were attacked by the land-hungry whites in a strange and terrifying new way.

The settlers used the law as their weapon.

Unschooled Iroquois found themselves the defendants in complicated law suits they couldn't begin to understand. Surveyors tramped over their lands whenever a boundary dispute arose. They were victimized by falsified deeds and rigged surveys. More often than not, the Indian rather than the settler lost in the white man's court of law.

In this critical situation Brant found he could be of service because he was in a unique position. He was Johnson's friend, and he was also familiar with the white man's ways and language. He became an official interpreter in the Indian Service, and helped his people get fairer treatment in land disputes than they would have gotten otherwise.

But even when outright fraud was avoided, the Indians were still under constant pressure to sell what bits of land they still owned. Brant began to realize with certainty that the westward movement of the settlers could eventually leave all his people homeless. Often he remembered Pontiac's warnings.

Despite these fears and the endless quarrels over land, however, the ten years just before the outbreak of the American Revolution were generally happy ones for Brant. As missionaries poured across the countryside in ever greater numbers, he became even more deeply involved in the Christian faith.

Sir William had long been a supporter of the missionary movement. He wanted to see as many English missionaries as possible traveling and preaching in the Iroquois towns. His reasons weren't entirely spiritual. It was obvious that if Indians would adopt the teachings of Jesus wholeheartedly, they would be more peaceful, much less of a threat to the Crown. In addition, the French were still sending priests down across the Canadian border. One way or another, France still wanted to keep its hand in colonial affairs.

So Johnson encouraged Brant's interest in religion. He watched with pleasure as Brant turned his home into a kind of unofficial headquarters for all the missionaries of upstate New York. Brant heartily welcomed the zealous young preachers from England. He spent long hours tutoring them in the Iroquois tongue, and even organized worship services at which he led the hymn-singing.

Still, Brant wondered about the way in which some of the whites practiced their religion.

He observed that they sang and prayed loudly on Sunday. But on Monday they were out trying to cheat the Iroquois of their land. It was discouraging, especially since Brant took religion seriously, and tried his best to live by the teachings of the New Testament.

During this peaceful period Brant remained in contact with the man who had really introduced him to the Bible. Schoolmaster Wheelock begged Brant to make a full confirmation of Christianity. Brant often thought about doing so.

In 1768, a great treaty council was called at Fort Stanwix, near where Rome, New York, stands today.

During October and November of that year, over 3,000 chiefs and braves of the Six Nations gathered at the fort to negotiate with Sir William Johnson. Johnson had long been trying to arrange such a meeting. Its purpose was to complete the transfer to the British of as much Iroquois land as could possibly be gotten.

Brant attended the great council. There is no evidence that he opposed the final terms of the treaty. He still trusted Johnson. Only later did he realize that, for the Iroquois, the Fort Stanwix treaty was a disaster.

When all the details were worked out, Johnson agreed to pay the equivalent of just over 10,000 British pounds in money and trade goods. In return, the English were given absolute ownership of all the Iroquois land south and east of the Ohio River. This consisted of the present states of West Virginia and Kentucky, and the western part of Pennsylvania.

Among the white men who took part in the Stanwix council were several powerful men from Virginia and Pennsylvania. One of these, Pennsylvanian George Croghan, was a good friend of Johnson's. In return for Croghan's role in helping persuade the Indians to sign the treaty, the King rewarded him with 100,000 acres on beautiful Otsego Lake, near present-day Cooperstown, New York.

Croghan had been one of the pioneer traders who traveled among the western Indian villages at the time of Brant's boyhood. There is no record that Brant ever met Croghan in those early years. But he saw him often at Johnson's home. When Croghan began to build a vast estate at Otsego, Brant was invited to visit there.

Croghan named his new domain Croghan Forest. The place swarmed with craftsmen putting up houses and a mill. New roads would connect the wilderness estate to other villages. Brant saw no great threat to the Indians in all this bustle of activity. Instead, he was pleased to share Croghan's hospitality, and to be treated—at long last—just as though he were an important white man.

Across the lake from Croghan's holdings was a home belonging to a young man named Lieutenant Augustine Prevost, the son of a noted English general. He had been educated in Europe, had lived in Switzerland, and was married to Croghan's daughter Susannah. In the young man Brant found a new friend. Prevost was an intelligent, cultured man of the world. And, to Brant's surprise, Prevost accepted the Mohawk visitor as a complete equal.

Brant went to Otsego Lake often during the next few months, sharing Prevost's food, taking part in lively talk about religion, and listening, fascinated, as Prevost described life in Europe. Brant very nearly forgot that he was an Indian at all. He thought of himself as a true citizen of the British Empire. This was where he belonged. This was the life for which he was suited. The illusion shattered when Prevost was abruptly recalled to duty in Europe.

Brant was reported to be "prostrate with grief." He was shocked to discover that the young officer was considerably less upset.

For Prevost, Brant had been an interesting, pleasant acquaintance, nothing more. The happy year of visits at the house by the beautiful lake ended as abruptly as it had started. Brant was forced to face the truth. He was not a European and never would be. Much as he wanted to live the white man's life to the full, he could not.

Prevost's departure marked the end of a period in Brant's life that had begun when he first walked through the door of Wheelock's school. How foolish, to think that he could ever be anything but what he was—a Mohawk.

In 1772, Brant's wife, Christine, died of tuberculosis. Finding the house at Canajoharie too grim, he moved to Fort Hunter. There he began to work closely with John Stuart, a minister of the Church of England. They started to translate the Gospel of St. Mark into the Iroquois tongue.

During this time Brant married his wife's half-sister. He was having more and more trouble controlling his son, Isaac. The boy showed every sign of being a typical Indian youth. He resented his father's discipline and demanded that he be allowed to do exactly as he pleased, even when that included teasing smaller children and torturing animals. He also blamed Brant for his mother's death. Brant hoped his new wife would be able to calm the boy down.

In 1773 Brant had occasion to visit Pittsburgh. He was horrified by what he saw there. The mud

streets of the small frontier town swarmed with settlers in crude wagons—and more seemed to arrive
every day. What was worse, these settlers were only
making brief stopovers before moving on west. They
meant to find new homes in the country beyond the
Ohio.

But the Iroquois had not given away that land in
the Fort Stanwix treaty! The settlers were supposed
to stay east of the river!

Returning to Johnson Hall, Brant pleaded with
the great man to make sure the treaty was honored.
It was not right for the English king to let settlers
move west of the line! The treaty clearly named that
area as the property of the Indians.

By now Brant's good friend was nearly sixty. His
step was not as quick, nor his voice as firm, as it
once had been. Already he was turning over some
of his affairs to his son, Sir John, and his son-in-law,
Colonel Guy Johnson. Both men lived at Johnson
Hall, though their having the same last name was a
coincidence.

But Sir William listened closely to Brant's plea.
He also paid attention to Brant's veiled threat that
the Iroquois would not take kindly to continued vio-
lations of the treaty line.

Johnson agreed to do what he could. He would
do this, he said, because Brant was his friend, and
also because Brant was an important leader of his
people.

Again, Brant realized his growing responsibilities.

How could he have been so foolish as to think of living as a white man? The Six Nations needed him. And Johnson made him realize it anew.

True to his word, Johnson sent a letter to England. He received a reply which assured him that the King was completely in favor of seeing the treaty line maintained.

Having seen the settlers streaming through Pittsburgh, Brant was not so sure that the King's assurance was worth much. When the grand council of the Iroquois met in the fall of 1773, Brant was there, speaking eloquently. He warned the Indians of the continuing need to resist the influx of white men. When he spoke, he spoke as a recognized leader. The chiefs listened.

Before the year was out, Brant's second wife died. Again the cause was tuberculosis. The disease seemed to strike hard at the Indians.

Brant had children to raise. This meant he still needed a wife. His choice this time would prove a lasting one. He was thinking of marrying Croghan's Indian daughter, Catherine. Since he had first seen her at Lake Otsego, she had grown into an intelligent and beautiful woman. Yes, Catherine might indeed be the right one. . . .

In the winter of 1773–1774, disturbing news drifted in from the cities on the coast.

The colonists were beginning to speak harshly about high taxes levied by the Crown. In December of '73, a group of citizens dressed as Indians boarded

ships in Boston harbor and threw cases of tea overboard, protesting a new tea tax. There was even some talk of open rebellion.

Brant questioned Johnson about this. Sir William replied that there was indeed a possibility of revolution. As friend to friend, however, he hoped that if the colonists did foolishly take up arms, Brant would keep his people loyal to the King.

It was a great deal to ask, especially since more

and more Indians were appearing at Johnson Hall to complain about the steady stream of settlers violating the treaty line.

To try and deal with some of these complaints, Johnson called a grand council at his house during the hot days of early July, 1774. About six hundred warriors gathered.

Even though he had been ill with dysentery for several days, Johnson insisted on standing up in the blazing sun and giving a rousing speech. He promised again to make certain that the treaty line was observed and the Indian lands protected. At the conclusion of the speech, Johnson presented a gift to the aging war chief of the Six Nations, Little Abraham. His face shone with perspiration as he sat down.

When the council broke up to eat, Johnson started back to the house and collapsed. That night, July 11, 1774, Johnson summoned Brant to his deathbed.

His message was brief and to the point: "Control your people."

Shortly, the great man fell into a coma. He died before dawn.

Now Brant faced an even bigger task. He must protect his people's rights without Johnson's help.

And if there were a rebellion, he would have to help make the decision about whether his people should support the King.

There was no doubt in Brant's mind that this awesome responsibility would fall to him. The settlers were already speaking of him as "the uncrowned king of the Iroquois."

five The Revolution Begins
1775

The death of Sir William Johnson left a huge gap in Brant's life. He owed much to the great man: his education; his first chance to test himself in battle; and much of his experience. His sister Molly took the loss equally hard.

She was invited to remain at Johnson Hall, which had been inherited by Johnson's son, Sir John. She refused because the house held too many memories. Sir John made arrangements for her to return to the original home she had shared with his father. There servants would look after her, Johnson's son said, for as long as she lived.

Sir John was equally kind to Brant. He told Brant that he could stay at Johnson Hall as long as he wished. Brant thought seriously of going back to Fort Hunter. There he could continue helping the missionary Stuart spread the gospel.

But Brant was too important a figure in the Six Nations to be allowed to waste his talents. Both Sir John and Colonel Guy Johnson, the newly named Superintendent of Indian affairs, knew it. Colonel Johnson pleaded with Brant to take a position as his assistant.

Brant wanted to know what sort of work he

would be required to do. Colonel Johnson said that the job would be something like that of a personal secretary. Many letters and official documents had to be translated into the Iroquois tongue. In addition, Brant would be in a position to help his people by giving advice to the superintendent.

Though he might have preferred to go back to missionary work, Brant realized what his duty was. He was now in his early thirties, near the peak of his manhood, and he still had the ear of the Johnson family. There was no doubt that the Iroquois needed every bit of help they could get if they were to hold onto their land and keep from starving. Brant accepted Colonel Johnson's offer, and agreed to live at Guy Park Manor, the colonel's home built on Sir William's property on the river.

There was one important piece of unfinished business to be taken care of before he started work. Lately he had thought a lot about Croghan's daughter, Catherine. He at last decided to propose marriage. When she accepted, he was overjoyed.

After the ceremony he bundled his new wife and his two children by his first marriage into a splendid canoe and took to the river. When they arrived at Guy Park Manor, Catherine was warmly welcomed. Brant believed things might be taking a turn for the better at last. Catherine was gentle but firm with the children. She seemed able to keep Brant's rebellious son under control.

Brant went to work enthusiastically. He enjoyed

his new duties. The superintendent sent him on several trips to the western Iroquois tribes, and Brant discovered again that he was held in high regard. His reputation was known everywhere. He was welcomed as a warrior who was a cut above most because of his education and position.

As 1774 ended, Brant read dispatches dealing with a possible war of rebellion. The dispatches arrived at Colonel Johnson's house almost daily. Brant couldn't quite believe them. He knew the strength of the King's armies. The colonists would never dare rebel!

April, 1775, helped change his mind.

Word traveled west to Guy Park Manor that small bands of colonists—now calling themselves patriots —had fought British soldiers at Lexington and Concord in Massachusetts. Even more surprising, the patriots had driven the British back to their camp in Boston and bottled them up!

At once, the British began fortifying Boston for a siege. The patriot forces were swelled by volunteers coming in from all parts of the colonies. Brant noted that some of the farmers from the Mohawk Valley had left to join the rebels. This troubled him. But still he did not think that the fighting would go on for long, Guy Johnson's fears to the contrary. Meantime, life in the Mohawk Valley remained generally peaceful, except for occasional arguments between settlers who sided with the patriots and those who were loyal to the King.

Events of mid-June, 1775, however, finally convinced Brant that war was likely.

Both the British and the American forces had been building up their strength around Boston for some weeks. On June 17, the British stormed the American fortifications on Breed's Hill. After absorbing terrific losses during the first two charges up the slopes, the British reached the top on the third and swept the Americans off.

A second, even more decisive victory was scored at nearby Bunker Hill. The patriot forces went into retreat. It had been a bloody victory. The King's men counted more than one thousand dead.

The impact of the Battle of Bunker Hill was felt immediately all along the frontier. Brant noticed the sudden feverish increase of attempts to get promises from his people. It was no secret that the side commanding the loyalty of the Indians in a war would have a big advantage.

In the middle of July, the American Congress hastily set up a special American Indian Department. Its specific task was to keep the Indians out of the war altogether. The Department was divided into three areas. The southern section included everything south of Virginia. The middle section contained the Ohio Valley. The northern section was responsible for all of New York, the area where pro-English sentiment was greatest.

Immediately after the Indian Department was organized, the head of each section received an official statement to be read to the tribes. It said, in part, "This is a family quarrel between us and Old England. You Indians are not concerned in it. We do not wish you to take up the hatchet against the King's troops. We desire you to remain at home, and not join either side."

From the beginning, both Americans and the British understood the entrance of the Indians into the war was all too likely.

For one thing, the Indians would naturally welcome a chance to strike back at their oppressors. (These might be the British or the Americans, depending on the point of view of the tribe involved.) And, to many of his people, Brant sadly realized, even if there were no good reasons to fight, the excitement of war itself was reason enough for going on the warpath.

The opportunity to loot and pillage the lands of the white men was a powerful lure. Johnson had understood this when he begged Brant to "control" the Indians. Brant wondered whether he could.

And if the Six Nations did go to war, on whose side should they fight?

The last question wasn't really hard to answer.

First, the farmers had been stealing the lands of Brant's people. And the farmers, as a class, tended to support the patriots. There were many more farmers in the Mohawk Valley than there were large landholders. These last, generally, sided with the King.

Second, Brant couldn't escape a feeling of tremendous personal loyalty to the Johnson family.

So he tended to think that if the Six Nations fought, it should be for the British.

The importance of Brant's opinion was clear from the flurry of letters he began to receive from his old mentor, Wheelock, who disagreed with the "stay-home" policy of the Indian Department. Wheelock was a patriot. He pleaded with Brant, in the name of their past friendship, to throw the power of the Iroquois behind the American cause. Brant replied rather sharply that, for years, he had thought of himself almost as an English citizen. In fact, he wrote, it was Wheelock himself who was responsible for this attitude. At Lebanon, Brant said, Wheelock had taught him "to fear God and honor the King."

Decided on his course at last, Brant waited for the opportunity to put his support and influence on the British side. He had thought it over and sincerely believed that protection of Indian lands depended upon the strength of the King. Historians agree that Brant also believed the British would crush the rebellion. It was just good sense to join the winning side.

Unfortunately, the British method of wooing the Indians in 1775 did not fit too well with Brant's plans. British policy seemed to be shaping up as a refusal to use the Indians at all, at least for the time being.

In late July Colonel Guy Johnson got an official letter stating that, "It is . . . his Majesty's pleasure that you lose no time in taking such steps as may induce them [the Indians] to take up the hatchet against his Majesty's rebellious subjects in America." But before many weeks were over, Brant realized that this stern cry for Indian support was nothing more than talk. No serious effort was made to organize the Six Nations into a fighting force.

Brant grew even more worried when certain missionaries showed their influence. Samuel Kirkland, the man with whom Brant once worked closely, got the entire Oneida nation to swear loyalty to the rebels.

Finally, to Brant's relief, Colonel Johnson decided to call a special Iroquois council.

The site he chose was Oswego, on the shore of Lake Ontario well removed from the Mohawk valley settlements. He picked the spot, he said, because he did not want to inflame the settlers. The council was held in an atmosphere of near-secrecy.

Around 1,500 Iroquois gathered. The chief representatives of the Crown were men active in Indian affairs—Colonel Johnson, John Butler, Butler's son Walter, and Daniel Claus. There was much speechmaking by the white men. But, to Brant, each speech was pretty much the same—disappointing.

The Indians were urged to pledge their loyalty to the King. They did so by shouting. Then they were asked to stay in their villages until they were officially called to duty.

Brant sensed the unhappiness of the chiefs when they heard the request. Brant himself was angry. The Iroquois were willing to take the warpath on behalf of the King. But the King, it seemed, was not ready for the all-out support of the Iroquois. Brant soon learned why.

Sir John Johnson's deputy, John Butler, was strongly against immediate use of Indians in the war. He argued that because the King's forces along the border were spread very thin, an American attack on Canada would be hard to repel. And Butler thought—probably rightly—that a string of Indian raids, and the cruelties that would be sure to go with them, would only enrage the Americans along the Lake Ontario frontier. This would surely bring on the feared attack on Canada.

Colonel Johnson did not completely share this view. But he respected Butler's opinion, because Butler had had a great deal of military experience on the frontier. For the time being, Johnson was content with making speeches. He did not throw down the war belt at Oswego.

Only one event at the council pleased Brant at all. Little Abraham, the Six Nations war chief, made a long speech in which he said that, because of his age, he no longer wished to take the warpath. But he knew the Iroquois would need a strong war chief in the days ahead. Therefore he proposed that the assembled Indians acclaim as war chief the one man who was obviously best fitted for the honor. The man was a Mohawk, as the Iroquois war chief always must be. The man was wise both in the ways of battle and of the whites. The man had the trust of the great Johnson family. The man, of course, was Thayendanegea.

Brant's selection was approved by a tremendous wave of shouting by the braves. Even older Mohawk chiefs who should have been given the honor ahead of Brant realized the wisdom of the choice, and added their voices to the others.

As the summer of 1775 drew to an end, the new war chief traveled north to the great city of Montreal. There he and Colonel Johnson met the Canadian governor, Sir Guy Carleton. The governor treated them with courtesy. But he made the same sort of wishy-washy speeches that Brant had heard at Oswego.

Yes, the King welcomed the loyalty of the Six Nations. But for the time being, in order not to bring on an invasion of Canada, the Iroquois were requested to stay home and do nothing.

Unhappy, Brant returned to the Mohawk Valley. There he discovered that news of the Oswego council had terrified the settlers, and started them arming for an immediate Indian attack.

News of what actually happened at Oswego and Montreal soon calmed their fears, though. For a few weeks the situation settled back to normal. A handful of Iroquois chiefs even went to Albany for a special conference called by the American commissioners. There they heard still more speeches asking for their neutrality. The Indians went away disgusted. Both sides were saying the same thing.

In September, however, the feared patriot attack on Canada came—with no Indian raids preceding it.

Brigadier General Richard Montgomery and Colonel Benedict Arnold marched to the St. Lawrence. The tiny British garrison at Montreal surrendered in mid-November. The Americans swept on toward Quebec. Governor Carleton fled ahead of them by night.

But John Butler still refused to call the Indians to war. Now he had a new reason. Since Canada had already been invaded, he said, it was a lost cause. The Indians should be saved until a time when their power could be put to full use.

Because of Butler's military experience, Sir John Johnson allowed him to make decisions in these matters. And the British high command abided by Butler's wishes.

But Brant was bitter about the ruling. So were Colonel Guy Johnson and his assistant, Daniel Claus. Both men had changed their thinking, and wanted to use the Indians immediately.

For this reason, Colonel Johnson and Brant decided on a daring move. They would go over Butler's head. They would appeal directly to the King's cabinet ministers in England!

In response to their letters the King wrote that they would be most welcome at his court.

six

Brant in England
1776

Brant was in England during the winter and early spring of 1776. The trouble in the colonies seemed unreal, even though London was talking about the wish of the Americans for an outright split with the mother country—a declaration of independence, so to speak. Brant was too busy to think much about the idea.

The government of his Majesty, George III, was arranging and paying for the whole trip. Brant and his party were met at the docks by the Secretary for Colonial Affairs, Lord George Germain. They were driven to their lodgings in Germain's great golden coach.

Brant looked out of the coach window and saw streets teeming with more white people than he had ever imagined. Hundreds, thousands of strange white faces seemed to swirl around him.

The coach rattled on to the Westminster district, where the Indians were to stay at a comfortable inn called The Swan with Two Necks. The sight of so many whites left Brant saddened and a little fearful. Perhaps he clutched his combination pipe and tomahawk a bit tighter as the coach wound through the streets.

Brant had brought the tomahawk along because it was part of the Indian finery he intended to wear at public gatherings. He kept it close by now because he had heard that there was a band of white men in London who made it their business to attack and rob visitors. The newspapers considered these robbers as savage as the Indians of the colonies, and therefore called them "Mohocs."

Once settled at The Swan with Two Necks, Brant began making official calls at the government offices with Guy Johnson. Lord Germain welcomed all the Indians politely. He promised to arrange an audience with the King as soon as the monarch's schedule permitted. But it was clear to Johnson—and Brant—that the other chiefs were of no interest to the King's secretary. Nor were their opinions. Germain really listened only to Brant, and paid tribute to his importance by calling him "King of the Indians."

This term was soon picked up by the press and the public. When Brant and the other chiefs went sight-seeing, crowds followed their coach. The people wanted a glimpse of the visitors in their animal-skin leggings and shirts.

Brant was fascinated by all the things he found for sale in London shops. He bought several broadcloth suits with waistcoats and breeches. He persuaded some of the other chiefs to buy similar outfits. They did, without much interest. But the people of

London were delighted by the "Mohoc" who appeared at parties in suits of the latest style.

Whenever Brant went into a shop, he felt the power of his long association with the white man's world. Here were things he could appreciate, things he wanted to have for his own. He bought himself a handsome gold signet ring and ordered special engraving for it. The finished ring read *J. Brant— Thayendanegea.*

All during his visit, Brant was entertained at parties in his honor, fussed over by members of the Colonial Affairs ministry. Obviously he was being courted because he was the spokesman for his people. He realized anew that if he could not deal with the King and protect the rights of the Iroquois, no Indian could.

At each of the splendid parties, he was the center of attention. Gowned ladies and waistcoated gentlemen crowded around him, eager for his promise that the "Mohocs" intended to remain loyal to the King.

Brant usually told them that the Indians were not only anxious to support the great King, they were anxious to fight for him. Perhaps one day soon, Lord Germain would agree to let them!

One of the high points of Brant's visit to London was his introduction to journalist James Boswell.

Boswell, a Scottish lawyer, was an important man in London circles. He had met Samuel Johnson, the famous dictionary-compiler, and become a member of Johnson's exclusive "club" of literary figures. Toward the end of the century, Boswell would write his famous biography of the great man. In the winter of 1776, however, he was most interested in the "King of the Indians." He arranged a meeting for supper.

To Brant's surprise, Boswell turned out to be a very uncolorful man. He was sober, even stuffy, and dressed in the dour black clothing of a poor scholar. But the Indian was delighted by Boswell's lively interest in American Indian life. The journalist wanted to know every detail. Like most human beings, Brant liked anyone who was a good listener.

The two ate supper together frequently during the remainder of Brant's London stay. They became genuinely good friends. Again Brant felt the tug of civilization. He was treated as a complete equal by this esteemed writer. He could hold his own with any white man! He could enjoy living in London the rest of his life. . . .

Still, there was always the nagging thought that he was responsible for the welfare of all the Iroquois, especially his own Mohawks.

Sometime during this visit, scholars agree, Brant finally made up his mind for good that he must put Indian interests ahead of personal ones. It was not a sudden decision, accompanied by claps of thunder and bolts of lightning. Rather, it was the gradual but final result of years of living with the problems of his own people—and of seeing the crowds on London's streets. After he returned from England Brant often said that his single strongest impression of that place was of the tremendous numbers of people. The more people, the greater the white man's power. Brant finally understood that he had to resist that power at all costs.

Although it was already the month of March, the audience with George III had not yet taken place. The Indians and Colonel Guy Johnson were growing impatient.

Brant was still a center of attention, however, The *London Magazine* published a long article describing his impact on the English capital. He was even invited to sit—uncomfortably, in full Indian costume—for a portrait paid for by the Earl of Warwick and painted by the noted artist George Romney.

Finally, toward the middle of March, Colonial Secretary Germain was ready to put polite talk aside and get down to discussing the real issues behind the Indian visit.

George Germain was an ex-soldier who had been stripped of his rank because of a charge of cowardice. His political fortunes had brightened lately, though. He was a strong supporter of the harsh anti-colonial policies of the prime minister, Lord North. Those policies had led directly to the outbreak of the Revolution.

Germain was all in favor of strong punishment for the colonists who had dared to defy the King.

It was Germain who was responsible for the hiring of paid German soldiers during the war. He also helped persuade Colonel Benedict Arnold to betray the American cause. All in all, he was a rather bloodthirsty nobleman.

In fact, Germain's eager cruelty was so well known that he was later criticized by men of his own country. One nobleman actually denounced him openly:

". . . Who is the man that, in addition to the disgrace and mischiefs of the war, had dared to authorize and associate to our arms the tomahawk and scalping knife of the savage? to call into civilized alliance the wild and inhuman inhabitants of the woods? to delegate to the merciless Indian the defence of disputed rights, and to wage the horrors of his barbarous war against our brethren? My lords, these enormities cry aloud for . . . punishment!"

Brant, neither "wild" nor "inhuman," was nevertheless able to see the secretary for what he was—ruthless. Germain was all in favor of immediately using the Indians to kill and burn. Guy Johnson had already learned this in private interviews.

Therefore, Brant decided, he could bargain with Germain.

He could trade the loyalty of the Iroquois for what the Indians wanted most—the King's promise that the Fort Stanwix treaty line would be observed, that no more Indian lands would be swallowed up by settlers.

Brant said to Germain:

"We have crossed the great lake, and come to this kingdom with our superintendent, Colonel Johnson, from our Confederacy, the Six Nations and their allies, that we might see our Father, the Great King, and join in informing him, his councilors, and wise men, of the good intentions of the Indians, our brethren, and of their attachment to his Majesty and his government. . . ."

Now it was time to bargain:

"Brother. The Mohawks, our particular nation, have on all occasions shown their zeal and loyalty to the Great King, yet they have been very badly treated by his people in that country, the City of Albany laying an unjust claim to the lands on which our Lower Castle is built, as . . . others do to those of Canajoharie, our Upper Castle. . . . We also feel for the distress in which our brethren on the Susquehanna are likely to be involved by . . . the Boundary we settled in 1768. Also, concerning religion, and the want of ministers of the Church of England. We have only, therefore, to request that his Majesty will attend to this matter; it troubles our nation and they cannot sleep easy in their beds. Indeed, it is very hard when we have let the King's subjects have so much of our lands for so little value, they should want to cheat us in this manner of the small spots we have left for our women and children to live on. We are tired out in making complaints and getting no redress."

Germain listened, then agreed. He would see to it that the land disputes were settled. But at the right time. That would not be until the end of the current rebellion, of course.

Brant had no choice but to accept this decision. He was pleased that he and Germain at least understood one another. And Germain promised that the Indians would be ordered into battle soon. This was the reassuring word Brant could carry back to America.

The audience with the King came at last. For Brant it was an anticlimax.

King George, though handsome, did not seem particularly regal. Brant was disappointed that

George wore no jeweled crown. And he did not think it was fitting for the King's people to nickname him "Farmer George" just because he liked to spend so much time at his country estate.

At the audience Brant once more pledged Indian loyalty. George pledged the Crown's continued "love" for its "children" in return. Brant went away thinking that he was just as much of a king as George.

During the first week in May Brant said his goodbye to Lord Germain. In part of his formal speech there is clear indication that he had now fully assumed the role of leadership. Without referring directly to himself, he made it plain that he spoke for all the Iroquois:

"Brother. As we expect soon to depart for our own country . . . we request you, and the great men who take charge of government, not to listen to every story that may be told about Indians, but to give ear only to such things as come from our chiefs and wise men in council."

This Germain would certainly do. And he would depend on Brant's word most of all. The chiefs prepared to sail.

Somehow, Brant did not feel the trip was a complete success. Perhaps it was because he saw the future too well.

He knew now that his people would have to take the warpath to uphold their end of the bargain he had been forced to make. Because he had been taught the Christian virtues of tolerance and mercy, Brant was not overjoyed at the thought of turning the Iroquois loose in battle.

"Control your people," Johnson the elder had told him. This he must do in the months ahead—at whatever price.

Then there was another troubling question. Would the King really keep the promise he had made through Germain? Brant wasn't sure. He knew the colonists would lose the war. But could the English be trusted afterward? There were just too many Englishmen. They could easily forget promises and trample over the Indian lands whenever they wished.

Unless—it was a daring thought—the Indians fought together, as they had never fought together before. Strange, this coming back to the idea Pontiac had tried to put to work. Perhaps he could succeed where Pontiac had failed. If the Indians fought as one people in the battles just ahead, the British would see how powerful they were—and would keep their promises rather than risk another struggle.

The dream of a united Six Nations filled Brant's mind in May of 1776, as he, Colonel Johnson, and the chiefs sailed for America—where total war was becoming more and more certain with every hour that passed.

Unity.

It was the only way.

Brant's dream of a powerful and united Six Nations lasted a little less than a year. It lasted from the time he first began to think seriously about the idea during the long sea voyage home, to the bitter winter of 1776–1777, when it died in the embers of a great council fire.

The year was the most heroic of Brant's life, and at the same time the most tragic. Like many another human being, he found himself a prisoner of his past actions.

Those past actions, above all else, destroyed his dream.

Just as Lord Germain did, the Americans thought of Brant as *the* Indian. He was the one who would bring war to the frontier if war came. Indeed, American eyewitnesses to the Battle of the Cedars in Canada in late May, 1776, swore that Brant had been the leader of a mixed party of Seneca, Cayuga, and Canadian Indians.

The Indians had been employed to frighten American officers into a quick surrender. (John Butler, still reluctant to release the Indians in an all-out attack on the frontier, considered this kind of Indian warfare "defensive.") The eyewitnesses said that Brant had run back and forth across the battle-field, waving his tomahawk and howling wild cries.

When the Battle of the Cedars took place, Brant, of course, was just preparing to leave London. But it was not surprising that many believed they saw him in Canada. To the frightened settlers on the frontier, "Indians" meant one thing above all—Brant.

He did not arrive in America until midsummer. By that time the Continental Congress had declared American independence. Brant learned of this development when he landed at Staten Island.

The island was British general headquarters. Sir William Howe's soldiers had moved down from Boston, and were preparing to try to drive General Washington's troops from their positions on Long Island and the island of Manhattan.

Hearing the news of independence, Brant decided that he must act swiftly to weld the tribes of the Six Nations into a single fighting force. To help persuade each tribe of the rightness of the idea, he needed to offer proof that England would win the war. So he stayed on Staten Island until the end of September, looking on as General Howe moved against Washington.

Between August 22 and 25, Howe landed about twenty thousand troops, including some of Lord Germain's Hessian mercenaries, on Long Island. He outflanked the positions of the American general, Israel Putnam, and attacked. Putnam suffered heavy casualties. When the Americans fell back to the heights of Brooklyn, Washington took over. He ordered a secret night retreat across the East River to American headquarters on Manhattan Island.

A retreat of this kind was exactly the proof of British superiority that Brant needed. In early September he set off for the Iroquois territory upstate. He traveled disguised as a white man.

Brant avoided the white settlements. Patriot feeling was already much hotter than it had been when he left. Also, there were now more American soldiers on the Mohawk frontier. When the Americans pulled out of Boston for Long Island, a few extra units of militia had been sent to reinforce American frontier posts like Fort Stanwix. The presence of American soldiers gave the settlers the courage they needed to turn against the British sympathizers— the Tories—with a vengeance.

It was wise for Brant to move through the frontier country carefully. Tories were being actively punished. Sir John Johnson had already fled to Canada, abandoning his father's huge home to looting by the American militia. Other outspoken supporters of the King had likewise made secret escapes across the Canadian border. And now, while Brant made his way north, people who were suspected of British sympathies were being persecuted. Their lands were seized. They were flogged, tarred, and feathered. Even hanging was not uncommon.

The Indians, too, were in a state of excitement.

Great numbers of Mohawks had left their disputed lands, to gather at Oghwaga, a safe village below the main Mohawk castles. In many of the other tribal towns—though not all—the talk was of war. The people hoped for a leader. They wanted to know who would win, Americans or British. They wanted to know which side to support.

Brant told them.

Everywhere he went during the remaining months of 1776, he preached the need to throw down the great war belt of wampum. Since returning from the Great King's presence, he had heard about how the British had driven the American invaders from Canada. He had witnessed with his own eyes the defeat of the Americans at New York! He could promise that the forces of the Great King would win the war. Hadn't he, Thayendanegea, seen thousands upon thousands of British men in London? A people so numerous couldn't help but emerge victorious.

In the western part of the Iroquois nation, the fierce Seneca listened to his oratory. They shouted their approval. Yes, war! War as a united people!

The Cayuga listened and echoed the Seneca. War! The Six Nations would fight for the Great King!

But the Onondaga were not quite so eager.

Brant met with them at their castle, also named Onondaga. It was the site of the great council fire of the Six Nations.

The fire was kept burning continuously. It symbolized the brotherhood of the tribes. The fire had burned for longer than the memory of any man who was there to hear Brant talk of the need to fight together to gain a strong bargaining position after the war was over.

Among the Onondaga, Brant began to hear remarks from the younger chiefs that brought painful memories of the past. Hadn't Brant talked against a strong union of the tribes when Pontiac put forth a similar idea? Hadn't Brant supported the white man then? Even now, some of the braves pointed out mockingly, he was not really dressed as an Iroquois. He came to them wearing the buckskin leggings, breechclout, and moccasins of a warrior.

But he also wore the cloth shirt and jacket of a white man.

Brant replied that he picked the costume for a reason. He wanted to show them that he was their best link between the white and Indian worlds. He could be trusted to guide the Indians wisely. The British trusted him, too. They had already made him a captain in their army!

Now, as war chief of the tribes, he demanded an answer. War or not?

Still there was grumbling, hesitation around the sacred fire.

Brant shouted that the Seneca and Cayuga were ready. So were his own Mohawks. He did not even have to ask them! Would the Onondaga refuse to go to war with their brothers?

The Onondaga chiefs at last gave their half-hearted agreement to fight. But Brant went away from the castle realizing that his past was catching up with him.

Wherever he went now, Brant carried with him

the memory of the questions of the younger Onondaga chiefs:

What guarantee was there that the British would keep their promises at the end of the war? Once the Indians had done their fighting, why wouldn't Brant's friends simply forget old agreements? If the Indians protested, the British could fight again. Hadn't Brant said that the people of London seemed numberless?

Of course Brant had wondered about all of this himself. His only answer was that the Great King had given his word.

The word of a white man?

Some of the Indians even said they didn't believe a word of Brant's claim that the British would win!

These were the questions that haunted Brant as he rushed on through the Indian towns. The fall grew chilly. The first snow flew. Already his bright dream was growing tarnished.

At the Tuscarora campfires it was even worse. The Tuscarora turned him down flat.

The reason was simple. Ministers of the Presbyterian and other non-Church of England faiths had gotten them to swear not to fight for either side.

Here was the past at work again! Brant himself— and Johnson!—had encouraged the missionaries to spread the gospel to the Indians. And this was the bitter result!

The winter deepened. Brant moved on to the

Oneida. He had already made up his mind that the decision of the Tuscarora was not important. They were not really one of the first five tribes. They had been admitted late to the confederacy. The Oneida, though, were members of the original Five Nations.

The Oneida also refused to fight.

At their campfires Brant's past came to life in an even more personal, painful way. It was the missionary Kirkland, whom Brant had taught and helped, who was mainly responsible for the tribe's stand. Without Oneida support, the Iroquois could not go into battle united.

Snow was flying now. Military activity was grinding to a stop as the coldest weather set in. Brant was faced with a terrible decision.

He had promised all his friends—Colonel Guy Johnson, Lord Germain, King George III—that he Iroquois would go to war for the Crown. But never in history had the Iroquois fought an all-out war unless every last tribe agreed. As long as this old rule was in existence, Brant could never fulfill his promise to the King. Therefore each tribe had to go its own way, make its own choice.

Gathering a party of Mohawk braves, Brant returned to Onondaga. With slow ceremony, he directed the putting out of the sacred fire.

Soon it was no more than glowing coals. Smoke drifted in the bitter December wind. The Six Nations were brothers no more. The dream of union was dead.

eight Battle at Fort Stanwix
1777

The colonists who lived through it called it The Year of the Three Sevens. Some called it The Bloody Year. It was the year in which Indian warfare began in earnest on the frontier.

As the year opened, Brant was still deeply shaken by the defeat of his great plan for unity. But he could not afford to waste too much time worrying. In the spring, he knew, a great many braves who had agreed to fight would be awaiting his command. It was his duty to see that they were organized and well supplied.

Early in 1777 Brant went on a special trip to Fort Niagara, supply headquarters of the British in western New York. Since his Indians fought with muskets, they needed powder. They had precious little at the moment.

At the Fort, Brant ran into John Butler again. He discovered that Butler was in charge of issuing all supplies to the Indians. And Butler was still opposed to letting Brant's braves fight. He would give them no powder.

Brant pointed out bitterly that Butler had allowed Indians to take the field in Canada in May of the preceding year.

Ah, Butler repeated, but that was a *defensive* measure!

It seemed like hair-splitting to Brant, and made him very angry. He demanded powder again. Again Butler refused.

Brant reminded Butler that the request came not from a mere Indian, but from a captain in the King's army.

To this Butler replied that Brant might be a captain, but *he* was a colonel. Also, he was in complete charge of the ammunition storehouse. The Indians would get no powder.

But the King had willingly accepted Indian support! Brant exclaimed.

The King, Butler smiled, was a long distance away. He also made a great many speeches. Some of the things he said were merely for the sake of making a good impression. Didn't Brant understand that? The decision was final—no powder.

Furious, Brant left Fort Niagara and headed straight for the safest place he knew Oghwaga.

Many of his Mohawks had been gathering there in recent months. It was to be Brant's stronghold. He meant to hold it at all costs, powder or not, because it was strategically located on the Susquehanna River, in the heart of the country the Mohawk had claimed for generations.

He found Oghwaga crowded. Too crowded for midwinter.

In addition to the Mohawk families that had

flocked in, several hundred Indians from other Iroquois tribes had settled at the fringes of the town. So had a hundred or so Tories who had fled the grim refugee camps that the British had built at Niagara and Oswego.

Through the cold months, word drifted out about the presence of the Tories. Their families came to join them. Women and children who had lived like animals, hiding and existing off the land since being driven from their homes by the patriots, swelled the population of the already overcrowded village.

The food problem became serious.

Hunting parties of half a dozen braves simply couldn't bring back enough food from the frozen countryside to feed everyone. Brant was forced to assign more and more of his Indians to the task. He thought about making a lightning raid on one of the American settlements to get provisions. But he didn't have enough men to make sure that such a raid would succeed. He was using every brave he could spare for hunting.

It was a harsh, frustrating winter. The war news was bad. General Washington had made a surprise march across the ice-packed Delaware River in late December. He had occupied the British stronghold of Trenton and captured over nine hundred Hessians, losing only five of his own men.

Somehow, the English flag that Brant had raised on a pole at Oghwaga seemed to flutter tiredly as the winter dragged to its dismal close.

The Americans on the frontier, meantime, were well aware of Brant's presence at Oghwaga.

Fear gripped settlements such as Cherry Valley, less than a hundred miles north of where Brant waited with his Indians. As the spring broke, the frontier seethed with weekly rumors of an Indian attack coming at this or that settlement. Small companies of volunteer militia began drilling in each village.

For his own part, Brant was disturbed by talk he heard among his Seneca, Cayuga, and Mohawk. They were boasting of what they would do when when they went on the warpath. Impatient to fight, they swore they would massacre every white man they encountered.

Somehow the Oghwaga Indians got hold of trader's rum. It made them all the more boastful, all the more eager for blood. When Brant suggested that they would have to fight as British soldiers did, some braves openly defied him. They would fight by their own rules! Brant began to wonder again how strong his control would be.

In the early spring he began to be genuinely worried about the horrors of an Indian uprising. For the first time his pledge to the King seemed perhaps unwise.

The patriots were equally afraid of Indian savagery—and of Brant.

The New York Legislature considered offering a reward for his death, spurred on by a committee report that stated that it was absolutely "necessary to provide measures for apprehending Brant . . . wherefore no cost should be spared for that purpose."

But rather than resort to a bounty, the Americans decided to try diplomacy first.

John Harper of Tyron County, New York, was an experienced frontiersman and ardent patriot. He was also a friend of Brant's. The two had been at the Lebanon school at the same time. Harper spoke fluent Iroquois.

The legislature sent Harper to see Brant at Oghwaga. A party of armed men went part way with him, but he left them at a nearby settlement and finished the trip with just one Indian guide.

The reunion was friendly. Harper tried to show his friendship for the Iroquois by putting on buckskin shirt and leggings, painting his face, and even taking part in a tribal dance. He handed Brant a letter stating the American position:

The New York Legislature—the "great council" as the letter put it—"will never suffer you to be defrauded of your lands; but will severely punish all who attempt it, and you may safely depend on our protection. . . ."

To prove the sincerity of the promise, Harper said that Brant would soon be receiving a quantity of gunpowder. ". . . We are not unmindful of your wants," the letter concluded.

Brant was honest with Harper. He had made a pledge to King George. On the other hand, he frankly admitted that many of the Iroquois wanted no part in the war. All they really wanted was the assurance that their lands would be safeguarded. This the Americans had certainly offered.

Brant wondered whether it was worthwhile to deal seriously with the colonists. If he did, he might prevent the horror and bloodshed of a full-scale uprising. He might also be able to make a better bargain on behalf of his people.

At the end of Harper's visit, Brant presented him with a special head decoration—a kind of crown made of a belt and decorated with beads. It showed that Harper was a trusted friend of the tribes. The giving of the gift was celebrated with a feast, after which Harper left. He reported to the legislature that the Indians were definitely going to stay out of the war.

To Brant it wasn't all that definite. He was merely open-minded on the subject now. Much had happened, many things had changed since he had spoken face to face with the King. He was willing to discuss matters with the Americans, provided they sent men with real authority to deal with him. Harper had no such authority and Brant knew it.

No American representative appeared. Brant grew impatient. He left the village with a party of eighty to a hundred braves, advancing up the Unadilla River. He was applying pressure—if the Americans wanted a bargain, they would have to act, and soon.

At the outlying farms, Brant demanded food for

his villagers. He even ordered several families to declare themselves loyal to the King or leave their land. A few of the families put aside their tools, seized those personal belongings they could carry, and rushed off to the safer settlements.

At last, however, runners reached Brant in early June with word that an American party was moving toward the Unadilla to talk, not fight. Brant's hopes rose. Then he learned who was in charge of the delegation.

Brigadier General Nicholas Herkimer was a well-known German landowner in Tyron County. He was also in charge of the local militia. With around four hundred men, he camped along the river and sent another message to Brant asking for a conference.

Brant knew very well that Herkimer did not have the power to speak for the whole American government. And, as a landowner, Herkimer could hardly be trusted to protect Indian rights. Annoyed, Brant kept the general waiting a whole week before appearing out of the forest.

The two met in a temporary shed erected in a meadow. Neither carried any weapons. There were the usual speeches. Herkimer urged the Indians to remain at peace. Brant pressed for promises about Indian land rights. The conference broke up at the end of June, having settled nothing.

By this time Brant was genuinely angry. It was an insult for the Americans to send a man like

Herkimer to deal with him. Later in life he often said that he would have kept the Iroquois at peace if the patriots had treated him with the dignity he felt he and his people deserved.

But they did not. Brant's braves slipped back into the forest to await the spilling of the first blood, which would take place in August.

In May of 1777, Britain's master plan for conquering America had been put into action.

General John Burgoyne landed in Quebec. He was to lead an army down the Hudson River, meet Howe near New York, and thereby split the rebelling colonies in half. Burgoyne had brought with him definite orders from Lord George Germain.

Butler's policy of restraining the Indians was at an end. In this great campaign, the tribes would fight.

As Burgoyne prepared to march south, plans were laid for a secondary British assault. A force commanded by Lieutenant Colonel Barry St. Leger was to strike out from Fort Oswego on the lake and take the American stronghold at Fort Stanwix.

Hearing the news after the June parley with Herkimer, Brant rushed north to Oswego. The Americans had refused to treat his peace offers seriously. Very well. He would personally command St. Leger's Indians in the march on Stanwix.

All through July, the army assembled its supplies at the fort on the lake. Sir John Johnson arrived.

So did John Butler and his son Walter, neither of whom Brant liked. Tories from Canada came in, too, eager to join the expedition and take revenge on those who had mistreated their families. The Indians danced much at Oswego. They drank and talked of bloodletting and booty.

The news from the east continued good. Burgoyne was still on the march. The Americans had abandoned an important fort, Ticonderoga, in the face of the advance. St. Leger advised Brant that once Fort Stanwix fell, his British and Indians would sweep into the Mohawk Valley and destroy it. Then they would attack the flank of the American army fleeing ahead of Burgoyne. Result—total victory on the New York frontier.

Word that a fearsome British attack force was being put together at Oswego raced through the up-state settlements. General Herkimer called for men "sixteen to sixty," and soon equipped seven hundred militia. He set out with this green, untrained army of farmers to relieve the garrison at Stanwix, which numbered only about 550 men.

St. Leger, on the other hand, had about 650 white fighting men, including regulars, Tory volunteers, and Hessian mercenaries, under his command. He also had eight hundred Seneca, Cayuga, and Mohawk in full war regalia, led by Brant. The general knew Fort Stanwix was running low on ammunition. It could not withstand a long siege. At the end of July, St. Leger marched from Oswego.

The army neared the fort on August 3. St. Leger was in for a disappointing surprise. Little more than a day before, a relief column of two hundred men had arrived at Stanwix with fresh supplies.

St. Leger presented his demand that the fort surrender. He included a frightful warning that of course he could not be expected to control his blood-hungry Indians if the demand were refused. His demand was met with calm defiance.

A strange new flag fluttered over the fort, Brant noticed. Someone said it had been adopted by the American Congress in mid-June. It was being flown on the frontier for the first time, this flag of red, white, and blue, with a design of stripes and stars. Perhaps it gave the defenders of the fort added courage. At any rate, they would not surrender. St. Leger settled down for a siege.

By nightfall of August 5, General Herkimer's army of green volunteers reached Oriskany Creek, about eight miles from the fort. Herkimer occupied an Oneida town—the residents had fled, afraid of the wild-eyed braves who had come with the British —and looked the situation over.

Herkimer soon discovered that he was outnumbered two to one. He wrote up a message to the fort's commanders. It asked them to rush out to his aid as soon as he engaged the British in battle. The fort should signal that they had received this message by firing a cannon three times.

During the morning of August 6, the forest was

silent. Herkimer's men grew restless. The general decided to advance—men, clumsy baggage carts, and all.

The day grew hotter. Herkimer's men refused to stay in ranks. They drifted off to the creek for a drink whenever they wished. Discipline disappeared entirely.

In the steamy late afternoon, Herkimer, riding a big white horse, was leading the column into a ravine about two miles west of the creek. It was hard for the baggage carts to maneuver in the ravine. The slopes were steep and densely wooded.

In the thickets on the slopes, Brant and four hundred Indians lay waiting.

St. Leger's scouts had kept good track of Herkimer's movements. Brant had slipped his braves into place for what was to be a typical Indian attack: the Indians could move swiftly; Herkimer's backwoods army could not. Brant waited, tense. Herkimer rode on down the ravine ahead of his men. . . .

Some of the Indians had been drinking. Impatient, they started shooting before Brant gave the signal. The trap was sprung too soon.

Even so, about two-thirds of Herkimer's force was caught.

The Indians howled, slaughtering the volunteers in the ravine with musket fire. Herkimer's officers died one by one. Herkimer's horse was shot from under him, and the general himself suffered a serious leg wound from which he would eventually die.

When the Americans in the rear of the column retreated in terror, small groups of Indians broke from cover and ran shrieking in pursuit. Tomahawks rose and fell, wet with blood.

The remaining Americans took to the woods. They tried to match Indian tactics, firing from behind trees. But the Indians were prepared for this, too. Whenever a militiaman stopped to reload his gun, two or more Indians would charge him and murder him with tomahawks.

As the battle raged on, the green farmers learned how to fight in the forest. It was either learn at once or die. Soon they were putting two men behind each tree. One shot while the other reloaded.

But the Indians, spurred on by Brant, pressed the attack. It would have been a total victory if a sudden thunderstorm hadn't forced a halt.

The storm passed quickly. The Indians heard a new, frightening sound from the direction of the fort. Gunfire.

Herkimer's message had not been received by the time the ambush was sprung. But the fort's commanders heard the firing and immediately sent out 250 men. These men swept through the all-but-deserted part of St. Leger's camp that had housed the Indians.

Each brave had been given money and trade goods at Oswego. This had all been left behind in the camp. The Americans looted everything.

St. Leger came after them. The Americans from the fort retreated, while the survivors of the slaughter at the ravine piled into their wagons.

Herkimer's men had lost all hope of breaking through to relieve the fort. The general had lost two hundred of his seven hundred men. Another two hundred were wounded. The remainder were escaping south to the settlements by the time the sun set.

The battle at the ravine had brought no pleasure to Brant. He had urged his braves to treat the captured Americans in a merciful way but his pleas were ignored. More and more scalps were taken, often from the wounded. As St. Leger rallied his men to press the siege of the fort, the Indians discovered that their camp had been looted. This only increased their wish for revenge. The killing of the wounded went on—but worse was in store for Brant.

During the two days immediately after the battle, the Indians began to desert.

They went one by one, then in larger and larger groups. They told Brant they were anxious to hurry back to their villages to tell of their victory and show their scalps.

When Brant argued that this was a military expedition, abiding by military rules, the braves paid no attention. The victory was won! And an Iroquois did as he pleased!

Hundreds left, and the more Brant pleaded and shouted, the more defiant the remaining Indians became. Though Brant was their war chief, his braves simply refused to listen to him. And if they felt like leaving they did.

It was the old, old story Brant remembered from his own boyhood. A brave was praised, not criticized, for doing as he wished. No amount of explanation that the rules were different in a white man's war did any good now. The Indian force was soon reduced to half its original size. The garrison at Fort Stanwix continued to refuse to surrender. The Indians who had stayed with Brant began to dwell on the losses that the Indians had suffered in the fighting. This in turn led to more heavy drinking, and to slaughter of more white captives.

Several times Brant personally put a stop to these outrages. He still remembered Wheelock's lessons from the gospel. He saw no reason why an Indian who had won in battle should treat prisoners without mercy. But his was a lone voice. The Indians considered it perfectly natural to murder white captives in any brutal way that occurred to them.

The siege dragged on. Still more Indians went home. St. Leger was thinking about giving up. His scouts brought word that a new American relief column was on the way and that settled it. St. Leger gave the order for withdrawal. The long, straggling retreat back to Fort Oswego began.

One of the major frontier battles of the Revolution was over. The new stars-and-stripes flag still flew above Fort Stanwix. What had started as a British victory actually ended as a stunning defeat.

For Brant the defeat was a terrible and personal one. He had been almost totally unable to stop his braves from deserting, drinking and murdering. Repeatedly his attempts had failed. He was a weary and unhappy man, this thirty-five-year-old war chief. And he had learned another bitter lesson.

The gulf between whites and Indians could not be bridged. His people could never learn to fight the white man's kind of war. His dream of a mighty, organized Iroquois army had been proved foolish by the behavior of the Indians at Fort Stanwix.

Quite naturally, out of Brant's bitterness came a desire for revenge against the people who had brought about this failure—the Americans.

He vowed he would not give up. He would strike and burn the frontier. He would make the Americans curse the day that Joseph Brant became their enemy.

nine *Brant Strikes*
1777–1778

After the disaster at Fort Stanwix, St. Leger split his army. He sent his regular soldiers back to Canada. John Butler took his men—Tory volunteers who made up a unit now called Butler's Rangers—to Fort Niagara to wait out the winter. The spring would bring a new opportunity to make war. And this time, Butler had decided it would be total war.

If the King had overruled him, had said that the Indians should be used, he'd use them. He'd use them to the full to spread terror and ruin—particularly in the Mohawk Valley.

The valley was important because its farms provided much of the beef and wheat for Washington's army. If the farms in the valley could be destroyed, it would help the British cause tremendously.

During the winter of 1777–1778, Brant got ready for the spring campaign by making a long tour through the Iroquois towns. There he recruited Indians to his cause. He had about the same luck as before. Those tribes that had listened to him still had plenty of braves eager for the warpath. Those tribes that were being kept out of the fight by the missionaries did not respond to his plea for volunteers.

But Brant had no trouble getting enough men for a sizable war party. As spring came in 1778, he returned to his base at Oghwaga, and waited for the right moment.

John Butler, a fat, unhealthy man well into his fifties, came to Oghwaga with his Rangers in late May. He had some good personal news to report. During the winter, his son Walter had gone out to gather men for his father's Rangers. He had wandered too far into American territory, and been captured. But in late April, John Butler told Brant now, Walter had escaped. And the elder Butler was eagerly looking forward to the day when Walter would take over command of the Rangers.

He was getting too old for frontier fighting, John Butler said. But Walter was young, a firebrand! The Rangers would be in good hands when Butler senior was forced to retire from active service.

To this outpouring Brant had no reply. He did not like Walter Butler. He considered him cruel and too hot-tempered. He hoped sincerely that he would never find himself serving under the younger man.

With this news out of the way, Butler outlined his plan for the spring attacks. Brant was to make a series of lightning raids up and down the frontier. The settlers would be thrown into a panic, wondering who would be hit next. In the confusion, Butler and his men would attack the American stronghold in the Wyoming Valley in northeastern Pennsylvania.

Brant agreed to the plan and the men parted. As May drew to an end, Brant struck.

With between three and four hundred Indians, he descended on the hamlet of Cobleskill on May 30. He set fire to a number of farmer's homes. But the fray was interrupted by the arrival of some American troops on their way to reinforce Fort Alden at Cherry Valley.

Brant's braves—dressed in the usual Iroquois war costume of moccasins and breech-clout, their faces and bodies hideously painted with slashes of red, green, and blue—killed sixteen to twenty of the troops. The settlers fled. Brant left Cobleskill burning and retreated into the woods. Smoke rose to the sky. In the fields lay dead horses, cows, and sheep.

Normally this kind of war party would have disappeared completely in the forest, not to be heard from again for weeks or months. Brant's method was different. He meant to conduct a fast-moving campaign, untypical of Iroquois warfare.

Because he knew the country, and could now find plenty of food for his men, he did not have to return to a camp for provisions. He could attack, retreat, attack again wherever he chose.

He knew this kind of a pattern of sudden surprise raids would drive the settlers wild with fear. They would begin to wonder whether, some sunny morning, *their* farms would be attacked by screeching Iroquois pouring out of the nearby woods.

The campaign of terror worked exactly as Brant and Butler had planned.

After Cobleskill, Brant attacked Springfield, just a short distance above Otsego Lake. A report sent to Governor Clinton of New York tells the kind of raid it was:

"Houses, barns, even wagons, ploughs, and the hay cocks in the meadows at Springfield were laid in ashes. Fourteen men were carried away prisoners, and eight killed. All the provisions were taken on horses, and carried off. Two hundred creatures (horses and chiefly cattle) were driven down the Susquehanna. . . . All this has been done while the garrison at Cherry Valley did not know anything about an enemy."

The last sentence proves the swiftness with which Brant struck. The Cherry Valley fort was no more than four miles from Springfield. All the woodland skills Brant had learned as a boy were serving him well.

The report to Clinton included a warning that Brant's raids were already putting the settlers "into the greatest consternation; they speak of nothing but flying off. . . ."

After Springfield, Brant burned Andrustown near Otsego Lake. At Andrustown he was hotly pursued by the local militia. He and his Indians escaped. The militiamen were so angry that they burned up the homes of several suspected Tories. Perhaps, off in the forest planning his next raid, Brant laughed.

During June and July Brant moved up and down the Mohawk frontier in these hit-and-run attacks. In late June he had to release a large number of his braves so they could return to Unadilla, where Butler was preparing his Wyoming strike. But even with fewer men, Brant continued to do his job so well that Butler's embarkation down the Susquehanna in boats and rafts was hardly noticed.

It was Brant the Americans feared, because they had heard what Brant had said: "I mean now to fight the cruel rebels as well as I can."

During these first months of the frontier campaign, Brant managed to keep his Indians from acts of cruelty and murder. True, his braves killed nearly three hundred soldiers and settlers in June and July. But these had all been men with weapons, fighting back. Brant allowed no killing or torture of prisoners. In fact, after a raid, his custom was to take prisoners along with him for a few miles, talk to them sternly about how bad it was to betray the great King, then let them go.

Part of Brant's success in controlling his Indians was due to the simple novelty of going to war at last. For the time being, burning white homes and tomahawking white soldiers seemed to satisfy the braves' thirst for blood. Brant hoped it would continue to be so. He did not want to go through the horrors of a Fort Stanwix again.

John Butler arrived in the Wyoming Valley in early July. He had about one hundred Rangers and five hundred Indians. They quickly captured two outlying stockades. At once a band of 450 militiamen marched out from the valley's main fort.

Butler set fire to outlying stockades. The Americans assumed he was retreating, and charged after him. That was just what Butler wanted.

He unleashed a surprise attack by his Indians who were lying in wait in a patch of marsh. The Americans were trapped. They turned in panic. The Indians went after them, shooting, clubbing, spearing, tomahawking. Estimates of the American dead ranged from 225 to 400.

On July 4, the main fort surrendered. Butler himself kept his Indians restrained. No eyewitness ever reported that Butler allowed a single settler, settler's wife, or child, to be killed once the surrender was official.

And yet, after the settlers were released and allowed to leave the valley, they told hysterical stories of the vilest, bloodiest Indian atrocities that could be imagined. Somehow or other, the historical record became confused. Butler was called a butcher. Tales spread throughout the colonies about the awful Wyoming "massacre."

And to cap it all, Brant, who had been busy in New York all the time, was named as the leader of the Indians at Wyoming.

For years afterward, historians insisted that Brant

had fought there, and had inspired his Indians to commit all sorts of dreadful deeds. The truth did not really matter to people whose nerves and tempers were inflamed by war. Brant's reputed role in the Wyoming "massacre" was just another proof of his savagery.

During his retreat to Niagara, John Butler fell ill. He transferred command of the Susquehanna district to his aide, William Caldwell. Caldwell and Brant decided to continue the program of attack-and-retreat. Now was the time to deal a serious blow to the important sources of food for Washington's army.

The target, in late summer, was the rich riverside farming area of the Mohawk Valley called German Flats. The settlers spelled it Flatts. For weeks the residents had been fearing an Indian raid. Scouts were sent out in all directions.

Brant moved on the Flats with some 300 Tories and 150 Indians. Four scouts observed his coming.

Brant's Indians caught and killed three but one escaped. The man ran for hours to carry a warning back to the settlement.

By the time Brant arrived at German Flats on the morning of September 17, all of the settlers were safely barricaded in two forts beside the river. There was some talk of the local militia going out to fight, but the militiamen were too frightened. So the settlers were forced to watch as Brant's men moved up and down the river banks, carrying off everything they wanted and burning everything they didn't.

An American report on the raid stated that Brant's braves destroyed sixty-three farmhouses, fifty-seven barns, three mills for grinding grain, plus a sawmill. They took hundreds of horses, cattle, and sheep.

Brant faded into the wilderness again, leaving the settlers angry and disheartened. There seemed to be no way to fight this Indian who came and went like a ghost!

Finally, though, the American authorities were starting to understand that they could not fight a frontier war on *their* terms. They could not meet the enemy at a place of their own choice. They had to destroy Brant the way he was destroying them— by attacking the Indian supply bases, the villages.

An American expedition headed by another Butler—Colonel William, no relation to John and Walter—set out to do that in late September.

William Butler's several hundred men were discovered by Indian scouts, however. By the time the Americans got to Oghwaga, all the braves had fled.

Butler described Oghwaga as "the finest Indian town I ever saw." That didn't stop him from burning and looting it. Some thirty to forty houses went up in smoke, together with all their contents. The nearby cornfields and granaries were also torched. There were vile atrocities, too, of which Brant shortly learned.

William Butler repeated this kind of attack on Unadilla on October 10 and 11. There he destroyed an estimated four thousand bushels of grain, much of it intended to supply the Indians through the long winter ahead. The expedition marched back to the Schoharie settlement, imitating Brant's tactics by taking along captured horses and cattle.

Runners fanned out through the forest to find Brant and tell him of the devastation. He appeared within a week, gazing in horror at the ruined homes and the destroyed grain.

And then, Mohawk women came to him with stories of how they had been molested and abused by some of William Butler's soldiers. This sent the Mohawk chief into a rage.

He did not allow his braves to commit such acts! Why, then, should the American commanders allow their men to hurt innocent people? It was a bitter thing to realize that all his efforts to keep his Iroquois from brutalizing women and children did not earn his own people equal treatment.

So far Brant's record was spotless. He had waged war since October without once being accused of excessive brutality. (The Wyoming "massacre" was the sole exception, and this story, as has been noted, was not true.)

But now the braves with Brant were in no mood for any more lectures on humane treatment of captives. They saw the ruin of their homes, heard the tales the women told, and muttered much about revenge.

In late October, Brant met Walter Butler on the

Susquehanna. As his father had predicted a few months earlier, Butler was now in command of the district.

Walter Butler proposed an immediate attack on Fort Alden at Cherry Valley. Some historical records say he did this merely because he was a good military commander, and believed that the American attacks on Oghwaga and Unadilla should be punished at once. Other historians maintain that Butler—a cruel man as Brant already knew—was hungry for revenge against the Americans because he'd been badly treated while a prisoner.

Either way, Walter Butler argued for a prompt attack. He wanted Brant to supply the Indians.

Brant was reluctant. He did not want to serve with Butler. Further, it was almost wintertime. The keen fall air of upper New York had already been darkened several times by snow flurries. It was customary for Iroquois to end their fighting in time to return home before the first snow. This way, they would be ready to trap and hunt in the winter months, to keep themselves and their families alive.

Brant knew it was going to be a terribly hard winter. The Indians would have to go somewhere besides the two burned villages—perhaps Niagara. He worried about whether there would be enough food.

But Walter Butler was insistent. Finally Brant agreed to go. Probably the fact that his braves too were eager for revenge had much to do with the decision.

Fort Alden at Cherry Valley was supposedly garrisoned by about 300 Massachusetts volunteers and 150 local militiamen, commanded by one Colonel Ichabod Alden. Walter Butler's force included 200 Rangers, 50 regular British soldiers, and about 400 Seneca, Cayuga, and Mohawk. The attackers would have to take Cherry Valley by surprise. There were other American units within a day's march of the outpost.

As Butler and Brant set out, the November weather turned foul, a miserable mixture of rain and sleet. Brant's spirits were low. He was exhausted from the months of guerrilla-type warfare in the forests. He noted that his Indians, originally eager, grew unhappy and quarrelsome in the cold, sloppy weather.

But Brant had given Butler his word. He kept his braves moving—straight toward the low point of his life, the Cherry Valley Massacre.

ten *Massacre*
1778

As the little army under Walter Butler neared Cherry Valley, Brant began to worry that there would be serious trouble.

Among the Rangers were a number of Tories whose families had been badly mistreated by the Americans. The Tories talked just as the Indians did—of revenge. The warlike Seneca, when not complaining about the wretched weather, were boasting that they would take many scalps. Their cruel smiles upset Brant not a little.

The leader of the Senecas was a huge, brutish-looking chief called Hiokatoo. Brant knew his reputation. Although married to a white woman who had been stolen from her family, Hiokatoo had a terrible hatred of most whites. This let him justify any act of cruelty, including tomahawking white babies. Brant was alarmed to hear the big war chief promising to do something similar at Cherry Valley. He hoped the battle would be over quickly. There were indications that Butler might be able to take the settlement by surprise.

For weeks the settlers at Cherry Valley had suspected that they might be in for an attack. On November 9, the fort's commander, Alden, was expecting the arrival of a relief column commanded by Colonel Jacob Klock. When Alden heard nothing from Klock, he sent scouts out.

Sometime during the night, Butler's advance guard surrounded the four American scouts who were sleeping at their sodden campfire. The scouts were taken prisoner. The fact that they had been caught sleeping was a good sign. It meant they believed no army—especially not one that included Indians—would travel in such bad weather.

The weather stayed bad: snow continually changing to rain and back again. On November 10, Butler stopped briefly when it got dark. He planned to keep moving during the night so that he would be in position to attack at first light. The rain began again. Grumbling, the Indians refused to go on.

Brant talked with them. It did no good. The army made camp for the night.

Brant circulated among the little clusters of men, listening to the threatening talk of the Tories and the Senecas. He did not like what he heard.

Before dawn on November 11, Butler ordered the army forward. Brant was with the advance guard that crept up the slope of a hill through dense pines, then took places along the crest overlooking the valley.

Below, Brant and the others saw the settlement spread out along Cherry Valley Creek. There was a scattering of houses. One belonged to Robert Wells, a settler he had known in the past. Brant's relations with Wells and his large family had always been friendly. He had to see that the Wells were not harmed.

The house of Robert Wells was a large one. Large enough for Colonel Alden and some of his officers to live there. They preferred it to the rude stockade some four hundred yards away. Even now, Brant saw smoke rising from the chimney of the house. Lamps glowed in the windows. An officer from the fort hurried to the doorstep and ducked inside, out of the freezing rain.

All through the morning the Rangers and Indians straggled up the hill and took their positions, muskets and scalping knives and war clubs and tomahawks ready. The Indians talked impatiently of wanting to start the attack. Every once in a while Butler had to repeat his order that there would be no firing until he gave the signal. He planned to strike right at noon.

An hour or so before that, two men appeared down near the houses. They were heading out with axes to chop wood. There was a sudden stir among the Senecas, an explosion of muskets. The Indians howled with glee as the woodcutters dropped, shot. Butler and Brant fumed. Cherry Valley was now warned.

Within minutes, Butler ordered the attack. Shrieking and shooting, the Tories and Indians broke from cover and raced down on the houses nearest the fort. Suddenly the door of the Wells house flew open.

Several officers, including Colonel Alden, had been having a meeting inside. At the first sign of trouble they started for the fort on the run. But they were too late. The screaming Indians and Tories were all around them.

Alden was tomahawked as he ran, falling dead in the cold rain. Rangers captured his second-in-command, Lieutenant Colonel Stacey. Threatened with death, one of the captured American scouts pointed out the other houses where officers from the fort were living. The search spread.

Some of the officers made it to the stockade. The gates were shut. One officer stationed outside the fort at the start of the attack, Captain Benjamin Warren, later described the next hours in a diary:

"The enemy pushed vigorously for the Fort, but our Soldiers behaved with great spirit and alertness; defended the Fort, and repulsed them after three hours and a half smart engagement. Twelve of the regiment beside the Col. killed, and two wounded. . . ."

With cannon in position to fire through loopholes in the stockade wall, the garrison would not surrender. As the afternoon wore on, Butler grew less and less able to maintain order among his troops. The freezing rain and slush made footing bad and vision worse. As the cannon from the fort belched now and again, the Indians began to slip away in small groups, then in larger ones.

Brant was roaming the settlement, trying to keep

all of his Indians in position to fire on the fort. Suddenly he heard a rumor that Hiokatoo had broken ranks and had started out on his own. Other Indians were roaming, too, particularly the Seneca.

Then came the most terrible word of all. Seneca had invaded the Wells home and slaughtered all the inhabitants.

Brant rushed to the house. Sure enough, it was true. The first atrocity of the Cherry Valley fight was also the most ghastly. All nine members of the Wells family, plus three white servants, had been put to death by gloating Senecas and a Tory Ranger. The Ranger bragged that he had split Mr. Wells's skull with a tomahawk while the latter knelt and prayed for mercy for his family.

Wells's daughter Jane had tried to run out of the house. She made it as far as the woodpile. She was caught by a Seneca who killed her with his tomahawk and then took her scalp.

Long after the massacre, Brant still grieved for these white friends. His deep hurt was echoed in the words of John Butler, ill at Niagara. When Butler heard the news of the Wells murders, he said, "I would have gone miles on my hands and knees to have saved that family, and why my son did not do so, God only knows."

Apparently Walter Butler didn't help the Wells family because he didn't know of the slaughter until it was over. He was still frantically trying to break

the defenses of the fort, and finding that he had fewer and fewer men as each hour passed.

Brant already saw signs that the massacre was going to be more widespread and horrible. Along the creek, other homes were burning. There were screams in the rainy gray air. Brant rushed up to a roving band of Cayuga and ordered them back to the lines. They paid no attention.

Brant hurried back to Butler's lines. So many Indians had left to pursue their own bloody pleasures up and down the valley, Butler actually had fewer men for the siege than there were in the fort. He had only his regulars, a handful of Rangers, and most of the Mohawks, who listened to Brant say again that they were not to run wild. They obeyed.

By late afternoon Butler knew his siege was a temporary failure. He gave the order to fall back.

With musket balls whizzing all around him, Brant rallied his Mohawk and organized them into a fairly orderly retreat. Butler led his troops to a nearby hilltop, and assigned positions. He was certain the men in the fort would soon rush out to counterattack.

But the defenders remained inside the stockade. It was enough to fill a man with contempt, Brant thought. This kind of cowardice was nothing new. Earlier in the summer, in fact, one American had actually written a letter to the governor complaining of "the unmanly dread which our militia entertain of these savages."

Certainly here was a good example of it. Many

of the settlers might have been saved had the garrison come out in force. Demoralized by loss of their senior officers when the attack began, they fought from cover all through the long afternoon.

As it grew dark, the Indians began to drift back with their prizes—clothing, bits of jewelry, bloody scalps, and huddled bands of terrified prisoners. The slaughter was coming to an end. Either thirty-one or thirty-two people died at Cherry Valley that afternoon—the records do not agree on the exact number. Brant was sick at the sight of so much blood. The arms and chin of Hiokatoo were smeared with it.

Though he could be a merciless enemy, Walter Butler did not approve of the killing any more than Brant did. And he was furious because the desertion of the Indians had undermined his plan for taking the fort.

As the Seneca and Cayuga arrived, Butler shouted at them, blaming them for failure to help him win a victory. Then Brant took over.

The toll was already enough! Twenty homes had been burned to the ground! Twenty-five barns likewise. The valley's two mills were in ruins. In addition, at least thirty people had been murdered! The Indians had not obeyed orders and the result was military failure and unforgiveable cruelty!

The Seneca were not impressed by Brant's anger. Their spokesmen argued that after Wyoming, the Indians had been falsely accused of every kind of bestial act. Well, they might as well go ahead and kill their seventy-odd prisoners since they would later be accused of doing it, anyway!

Butler and Brant both argued fiercely against this. Many of the prisoners, women, children, and older people, could not survive a long forced march to Niagara. Butler wanted these weaker prisoners released.

Hiokatoo and some of the other warlike Indians shook their heads. Had the Americans been kind and generous at Oghwaga and Unadilla? No! The prisoners would get what they deserved—tomahawks.

By now things were desperate. Brant spoke again. Finally, after heated speeches from both sides, the combination of Butler, as commander, and Brant, as war chief, silenced the opposition. The prisoners were guaranteed their lives.

It was only a small victory after all the horror of the afternoon. Brant took much of the guilt on himself. He should have known better than to try to mold his people into the white man's image. He had not succeeded, and the result was this slaughter.

Butler picked out the wife and four children of one Colonel Campbell, plus the wife and three daughters of a settler named Moore, for special treatment. He quickly sent a message to Governor Clinton in Albany saying he would hold these women and children hostage until Clinton released Walter Butler's own wife and children, imprisoned months ago, and the families of other Tories as well.

The prisoners were herded together and forced to spend the night without shelter on the soggy ground. Next day, Butler began to release the older ones.

Captain Warren's diary described the rest of the siege:

"Nov. 12—The Indians came on again, and gave a shout for rushing on, but our cannon played on them back; they soon gave way; they then went round the settlement . . . and collected all the stock and drove the most of it off. . . .

"Nov. 13—In the afternoon and morning of the 13th we sent out parties after the enemy withdrew; brought in the dead; such a shocking sight my eyes never beheld before of savage and brutal barbarity; to see the husband mourning over his dead wife, with four dead children lying by her side, mangled, scalpt, and some of the heads, some of the legs and arms cut off, some the flesh torn off their bones by their dogs. . . .

"Nov. 14—The enemy seem to be gone; we sent out to collect what was left of cattle or anything; found some more dead and buried them. . . ."

Walter Butler had raised the siege.

It was snowing hard by twilight on November 13. Butler realized that his men didn't have the heart to continue. The Seneca and Cayuga who had participated in the bloodletting were satisfied now. They complained loudly about the chilly snow. Butler was also worried that Klock's relief column would arrive at any moment. The column had been only twenty miles away the day before the massacre. Klock had chosen to move slowly. Perhaps it was another example of "unmanly" fear of the Indians.

The sad retreat through mounting snowdrifts began.

Brant hadn't wanted to come to Cherry Valley. Now he was sorrowing over the outcome. "Control your people," Johnson had said. Brant had failed again. It was a dark hour.

When word of the massacre swept across the frontier, it produced a new wave of horror and hate. Brant's name was mentioned every time as the one responsible for the butchery. It made no difference to the Americans that the facts again did not support the claim that Brant was guilty of inciting the Indians.

After some years, eyewitnesses did make it clear that Brant had acted with restraint. But as is often the case, people at the time believed what they wanted to believe. Everyone said Brant and Butler had let the Indians run riot.

In a letter to a superior early next year, John Butler even divorced himself from any connection with his son's actions—or lack of them—at Cherry Valley. He said: "The inhabitants killed . . . do not lie at my door."

Marching back to Niagara in the blowing snow with all but the sturdiest captives released, Brant guessed that his reputation was forever blackened. And the guilt was never to leave him. Later in the war, an Indian runner appeared with a captured white baby at the frontier headquarters on an American general. Brant had written a letter to the general in English:

"I send you by one of my runners the child which he will deliver that you may know that whatever others may do I do not make war upon women and children. I am sorry to say that I have those engaged with me in the service who are more savage than the savages themselves. . . ."

Brant faced the snowbound months at Niagara in a mood of despair and defeat.

eleven *Scorched Earth*
1778–1779

John Butler had now recovered enough to take command of the district again. He suspected that the Cherry Valley Massacre would only inflame the Americans into demanding that the Indian threat be removed forever. So, during the winter, while many of his people huddled miserably at Fort Niagara, Brant took to the trail again.

He was preparing for the spring offensive he was sure the Americans would launch. He pleaded with the reluctant tribes, especially the Oneida and Tuscarora, to join him in support of the Great King.

Once more the Oneida and Tuscarora said no. Brant returned unhappily to Niagara, to spend the remaining winter months with his wife and children.

Brant's daughter continued to be a delight to him. But his son, Isaac, growing into young manhood, was as unpleasant as ever. He openly defied his father's commands and made Brant's life miserable by his unruly behavior.

During the winter Butler sent Tory spies through the snowy wastes of upstate New York. The news they brought back was alarming.

As Butler and Brant had guessed, the settlers

were enraged about the Indian situation. They insisted that something be done. On February 27, 1779, the Congress acted. General Washington was told to take whatever steps were necessary to halt the terror.

Washington set up a special army to do the job. He put in command Major General John Sullivan, a New Hampshire lawyer who had served the patriot cause almost continuously since the start of the Revolution. Washington gave Sullivan sixteen regiments of regular soldiers, plus artillery and cavalry.

Sullivan's plan of attack was much like the one Butler followed in the Wyoming Valley campaign. He split his army. His own First Division would march north from Pennsylvania. The Second Division, led by Brigadier General James Clinton, would start from the Mohawk River and head toward the agreed-upon meeting place for the two armies—Tioga, on the Susquehanna River near the Pennsylvania–New York border.

At Niagara, Brant and Butler listened to reports brought in by scouts about the new army, and feverishly began assembling all the men they could muster. Brant knew that they would not have nearly enough. The invading force was said to be huge. By frontier standards, it was—all told, Sullivan had around four thousand men under his command.

Throughout the spring, preparations went ahead on both sides. General Clinton sent six hundred men to burn three Onondaga towns. It was a sample of the kind of war the Americans meant to fight.

In June Clinton started for the meeting point with his 1,600 men. He camped on the shore of Otsego Lake late in the month. There he waited for marching orders from Sullivan.

General Sullivan, meantime, did not get all his heavy baggage wagons and roadbuilding equipment moving until mid-June. By then John Butler and Brant had slipped out of Niagara. They headed eastward in slow stages. Butler had only about 350 Tory Rangers in his party. Sir John Johnson was with him, however. And Butler's son, Walter, was serving as his second-in-command. Along the route, Brant picked up as many Indians as he could get.

Brant was a full colonel now, courtesy of the British government. It did not mean much to him. Things were going badly. The Indians were slow to turn up at partially rebuilt Oghwaga, where Brant waited in late June. Almost daily, runners brought word of the advance of Sullivan's army.

The crop lands at Oghwaga and Unadilla were ruined. Brant had to take to the countryside for food. This he did, at the same time striking a blow he hoped would distract Sullivan's attention.

On July 21, having marched southeast with about sixty Indians and twenty-five Tories, he hit the Delaware Valley settlement of Minisink. But the settlers, fearing just such a raid, had already driven their livestock into the woods.

Guilt about Cherry Valley was much on Brant's mind. In a letter of report on Minisink written on July 29, he said:

"We destroyed several small stockaded forts, and took four scalps and three prisoners, but did not in the least injure women or children. . . ."

The Minisink raid immediately made the settlers cry for protection from Sullivan's army. He ignored the pleas, pushing on to Tioga where he arrived on August 10. Clinton's brigade was marching south from Otsego Lake to meet him. The two armies joined together on August 22. None of the minor summer raids like the one on Minisink could turn the American army from its course.

On August 26, the huge army turned west. Sullivan had left some soldiers to guard Tioga. A few wounded were being cared for there. But he still had nearly four thousand men. This enabled him to send scouts out on all sides, thus preventing a surprise attack, the favorite strategy of the Indians.

Butler was somewhere ahead of the Americans, with a total of about 750 men—400 of them half-starved Indians whose fighting spirit had nearly been destroyed by a bad winter and a summer without major Indian victories.

With so few men, Butler was forced to fall back on a strategy of surprise, even though Sullivan had a horde of scouts out in the field. Butler chose New-town, an Indian village about five miles east of present-day Elmira, New York. Here he would try to stop the invaders.

Newtown was located on the bank of a river. Nearby was a long, heavily wooded ridge that Sullivan's army would have to cross on its way west. Here, at the end of August, Butler and Brant prepared to make a stand.

A defense line was laid out along the ridge. The Tories dug trenches and put up breastworks of logs. Brant stationed his Indians around the left curve of the ridge. From there they could rush down on the flank of Sullivan's army.

All chance to surprise the Americans vanished on August 29. An hour before noon, Sullivan's scouts spotted the fortifications on the hill.

Sullivan, a cautious leader, did not launch an immediate attack. He took time to move his units into position at the base of the ridge. The key one was a brigade commanded by Brigadier General Enoch Poor. It was posted on the right flank of the main body of the army, ready to charge up the ridge and clear out Brant's Indians.

At about two in the afternoon, Sullivan ordered his artillery to open fire.

A thunderous roar swallowed the ridge. Sullivan was using howitzer shells. They hit in the woods

and exploded, sending metal whistling in all directions, crashing trees over, and setting branches on fire. Half a dozen three-pound cannon added to the din.

The rain of metal and the sudden crackling and roarings of limbs falling in flames terrified the Indians. They whooped and fired their muskets, but it was only a show. Some of them had never heard a cannon before. When shells whistled over their heads and landed behind them, they assumed they were surrounded. Terror became panic.

Poor's brigade advanced toward the ridge. Brant took some of his warriors and led an attack that sent Poor's men into retreat. It was only temporary. As Brant climbed back up the ridge, he saw Poor's soldiers coming on again, hacking their way through underbrush with their bayonets.

Soon those Americans would be in a position to outflank the Tory and Indian defenders. The trap would close. . . .

The awful cannon bombardment did not let up. The Indians behind the log barricades were talking openly of retreat. Brant kept them where they were.

"Such was the commanding presence of the great Indian . . . ," an eyewitness later wrote, "and such the degree of confidence he inspired that his undisciplined warriors stood their ground. . . . Above the roar of the artillery and the rattle of small arms could be heard the voice of Brant, encouraging his men for the conflict, and over the heads of all his crested plume could be seen waving where the contest was likely to be most sharp."

Brant knew enough about the white man's style of war to realize that the possible encirclement would bring disaster. He told Butler finally that retreat would be best. Sadly, Butler agreed. The Tories and Indians faded away from their hasty fortifications. Before long, the Indians were deserting again. They headed for their own towns to protect their families from the monster American army.

General Washington had given General Sullivan strict orders that prisoners were to be treated humanely. In fact, Washington had encouraged Sullivan to take prisoners, so that they could be used as hostages to prevent further Indian raids. But the woods around Newtown were empty.

In terms of numbers killed, Newtown was not a spectacular battle. Butler lost five Tories and Brant a dozen Indians. Sullivan's casualties were five dead and three dozen wounded.

But it was an important American victory. The roads into the Iroquois towns were now open and undefended.

Sullivan left his artillery and heaviest baggage behind. He moved swiftly toward the towns as the Indians fled in terror before him. He intended to destroy forever the war-making power of the Six Nations.

Sullivan scorched the earth as he passed.

Skoiyase—eighteen houses, cornfield, orchards burned.

Shenanwaga—twenty houses, stacks of hay, hog and chicken pens burned.

Kanandaigua—twenty-three "elegant houses, some framed, others log, but large and new," burned.

Gathtsewarohare was a village with vast cornfields all around it. In six hours two thousand of Sullivan's men burned every last acre.

Finally, on September 15, Sullivan reached the end of his fearful march, Little Beard's Town. This was the Great Castle of the fierce Seneca on the Genesee River. The flames carried away an estimated fifteen to twenty thousand stored bushels of corn.

Triumphant on the Genesee, Sullivan decided that his campaign had gone far enough. In a little more than half a month, he had wiped out forty-one Iroquois settlements—sent the Indians fleeing—totally destroyed the crops of the Six Nations—and had done so with a loss of only forty-one men. Four of these had died as a result of sickness, and two from accidents.

In another month Sullivan was safely back in Pennsylvania, a national hero.

The Indians who had fled from Sullivan's advance had no choice but to go to the British. Only the British could give them the food they needed to survive the winter ahead. They poured into Niagara at a record rate during the chill fall.

By all signs, it was going to be a bad winter. It was—the coldest the Indians could remember, and one of the very coldest in history.

From the days of the first hard freeze, the rivers became locked in ice. Snow fell at a record rate, making traveling and hunting next to impossible, even on snowshoes. Trees in the forest froze to their centers, and split open with loud bangs. Birds toppled out of the trees, frozen to death. Deer and elk perished by the hundreds.

At Niagara, Brant tried desperately to keep at least a glimmer of hope alive in the hearts of the pitiful refugee families. It was a losing battle. The Indians huddled in flimsy wooden huts hastily put up on the bluff overlooking the ice-choked Niagara River. Many women and children died of disease brought on by a lack of food.

By February, a few Seneca war parties struggled through the snow on snowshoes to attack and burn outlying settlements. Obviously, some of Brant's people still wanted revenge. But only some. The majority, homeless and hungry, were beaten.

In the spring Brant would lead the warriors again. He was still their war chief.

But he never again fought with quite the same heart or spirit. Newtown and Sullivan's march marked the beginning of the end of Indian resistance. The Revolutionary War on the New York frontier was all but over.

twelve "Do Them All the Good You Can"
1779–1809

With the surrender of the British army under Lord Cornwallis at Yorktown in October, 1781, the Revolution ended. So did Brant's last hopes of being allied with the winning side.

He had continued to fight through the closing years of the war. He led raiding parties in upstate New York, struck farms and forts and moved off rapidly to strike again. But Sullivan's march had robbed the Iroquois of their power to terrify on a broad scale. Brant's forays were only minor distractions.

At the suggestion of the British, he made a trip west in the summer and early fall of 1781. Supposedly he went to help fight the famous American frontiersman, George Rogers Clark. The expedition turned out to be little more than a loosely organized series of raids into Kentucky. Settlers were killed—among them, Daniel Boone's brother—but the military value of the effort was next to nothing.

At war's end, Joseph Brant began to worry in earnest about the fate of his own particular tribe.

The British had promised that the condition of all the Iroquois would be made "as it was when war began." Unfortunately the British were in no position to let the Mohawk return to their original New York lands. And Brant knew very well that the Americans would not welcome them if they went there on their own.

He made a trip to Quebec to appeal to the governor, General Haldimand. He pleaded so dramatically that Haldimand arranged for the Mohawk to be given land along the Grand River, a Canadian stream flowing into Lake Erie near its eastern end.

The other Iroquois tribes hoped to remain in New York, but the mood of the Americans was against this. The New York Legislature began to take steps that would end with all the Iroquois being driven out of the territory.

It was only the action of George Washington that prevented it. He favored a humane treatment of the defeated Six Nations. Gradually the tribes worked out their differences with the government. They were given small pieces of land in various parts of the state.

But Brant preferred to move with his people to a new Mohawk village on the Grand River.

There, for several reasonably peaceful years, he saw to the raising of his children from his first marriage, Christiana and Isaac.

Christiana married a young man of the Mohawk tribe. Brant even succeeded in finding a good-looking, good-tempered chief's daughter for his son. But Isaac was as hot-tempered as ever. He drank more and more every day.

Brant's third wife bore him children, too—seven in all, three boys and four girls. Though all the children had Indian names as well as English ones, the life of the Brant family was now completely civilized. It centered around a neat, two-story frame house in the new Indian town. The house was located in the midst of similar houses belonging to other Mohawk families. Some of the families did not like this style of living. But under Brant's leadership the little community developed its own farms, and the people did not starve.

The Brant house was made more lively by the presence of his favorite relative, his sister Molly. She was growing old now. She talked much of her memories of life with the great Johnson. Brant considered it a privilege to care for her.

But the Mohawk were always in need of financial help. Late in 1785, Brant decided that he should again visit England.

Once more he was welcomed as a celebrity. He was entertained at balls, receptions, and private suppers. He had a formal audience with George III. The King, as was customary, extended his hand to be kissed.

Brant remembered kissing the royal hand on his first journey to England. This time he did not move. He believed that his status among the Indians made him as much of a king as George III. Brant did, however, give way to politeness and kiss the hand of the Queen.

During the visit Brant sometimes wore English finery and sometimes a full Indian outfit. At a great costume ball given in his honor, he appeared fully garbed as a chief, with warpaint on his face. The ambassador from Turkey mistook Brant's painted face for a mask.

The story goes that the ambassador was so curious he touched Brant's nose. Seeing a chance for a good joke at a white man's expense, Brant leaped back, let out a warwhoop and flourished his tomahawk. The Turkish ambassador turned pale. Everyone else laughed.

A high point of the visit was the printing of Brant's Iroquois translation of the Gospel of St. Mark. Brant visited the offices of the publishers, the Society for the Propagation of the Gospel in Foreign Parts, and watched with pride as the books were finished. They were large and handsome. The English text was on one page and the Iroquois version on the page adjoining. It was a specially proud moment because the King himself had sponsored the project, and provided much of the money.

Brant did accomplish the main purpose of his trip, too. The Crown agreed to pay the claims that he presented for lost Mohawk lands. He was pleased when the government also agreed to listen to any Indian claims in the future. He returned home in 1786 feeling that he had done something to make up for the suffering of the Iroquois in general and the Mohawk in particular.

But a calm, peaceful life in Canada was not to be his quite yet. Spurred on by victory in the Revolution, the Americans were moving out of New York and Pennsylvania, through Ohio, and into the lands beyond. Brant saw the familiar pattern repeating itself—Indians being faced with loss of their land.

He made a series of western trips. He visited the lodges of the Ottawa and Wyandot, the Huron and Pottawattomi. He even went as far as the villages of the Miami Indians, who lived along the Wabash River in Indiana. His message was always the same:

The Indians must act together. Only unity gave them strength. The American government would not listen to separate tribes because separate tribes could always be beaten in battle.

The Americans soon got wind of Brant's activity. President Washington sent his commander-in-chief, General St. Clair, to hold a huge tribal council at the junction of the Muskingum and Ohio rivers.

Here, at Fort Harmar, the tribes—Six Nations as well as the western Indians, minus only the fierce Miami—listened as St. Clair proposed a series of treaties. These treaties would be signed individually by the various tribes.

Present at the council, Brant argued hotly against the whole idea. There should be a single treaty of peace with all the Indians, or none at all!

Despite his warning that the treaties were just a device to keep the Indians weak and divided, the majority of the tribes agreed to sign. Brant held the Mohawk fast. They refused to be a party to any agreement.

As soon as the council broke up, Brant returned to the Canadian village. He saw the white man's treachery reveal itself when St. Clair marched west with an army to wipe out the Miami Indians.

But the Miami were stout fighters. Under their war chief, Little Turtle, they attacked the Americans, killed over eight hundred, and sent the rest into wild retreat.

Because of this new threat to peace, President Washington invited Brant to Philadelphia in 1792. He wanted to discuss ways to prevent frontier war. Brant went to the temporary American capital with some fear. But he was courteously received, put up at a fine inn, and welcomed personally by the President.

Washington seemed really interested in the problems of the Indians. He promised that he would make sure all the tribes were treated fairly, if only Brant would help convince them that peace was in their best interests.

Though he did not trust most Americans, Brant believed Washington. He agreed to do what he could.

After leaving Philadelphia he made another trip to villages of the Miami. He urged that they give the President the chance to make good on his promise. Little Turtle would not listen. Brant warned him that one tribe had no hope of resisting the Ameri-

cans for very long. Still Little Turtle shook his head. When the American general known as Mad Anthony Wayne defeated the Miami in a great battle, Brant knew his warning had been right.

One great personal tragedy marred this later period in Brant's life.

At a summer council of the Grand River Indians in 1795, his son Isaac got drunk and attacked him with a knife. Brant disarmed his son and threw him down. Isaac jumped up again. Father and son struggled for several minutes. Somehow Isaac was slashed on his own knife.

Finally the drunken brave was carried away to a sick bed. His wound became infected. He died after four days.

Sick with grief, Joseph Brant went at once to the Canadian authorities and surrendered himself as a killer. The authorities refused to arrest him. They said Brant had clearly acted in self-defense.

But Brant felt overwhelmingly guilty. To punish himself he resigned his British army commission, from which he still drew pension money. The army refused the resignation.

Finally, Brant asked a council of his fellow Mohawk to judge the case and give a verdict. They did—not guilty. Brant felt only a little better.

Despite everything that had happened in the past, Brant still believed the white man's way offered hope for his people. Only through education could they free themselves of their traditional poverty and help-lessness. When he sent his sons one by one to be ed-ucated to Dartmouth College, he believed that he was doing a wise thing.

He commented in a letter to James Wheelock, Eleazer's son, that he wanted the boys "studiously attended to, not only as to their education but like-wise to their morals in particular." He thought of his education at the Indian school as one of the most important parts of his life: "Though I was an unprofitable pupil in some respects, yet my worldly affairs have been much benefited by the instruction there received. . . ."

In his older years, Brant was not forgotten by the King. For services to England, George III granted him three thousand acres of land at Burlington Bay on the shore of Lake Ontario. When he did so, the King sent his "regard and affection" to "his old friend, Captain [sic] Brant."

At Burlingron Bay Joseph Brant built a splendid two-story mansion with brick chimneys at either end. Here he spent the remainder of his life, traveling now and then into the new American nation to speak on Indian affairs.

He could reflect on a life that was a success or a failure, depending on how he looked at it.

As a father, he had failed in raising his son Isaac.

As a leader, he had failed in living up to John-son's plea that he control his people, though he had tried hard.

As a senior chief of the Iroquois, he had failed to bring about the realization of a great union of the tribes.

Yet he had won for himself well-deserved fame. As memories of Cherry Valley faded, the Americans came to regard him as a courageous and humane chief. He had learned well the Bible's lessons of mercy, and had put them into practice wherever and whenever the perilous times permitted.

In the late fall of 1807, at his Ontario home, Brant was stricken with the ravages of old age. Though just sixty-five, he had lived several lifetimes of suffering. He was feeble now, wasted away.

On November 24, he called his wife and his sister Molly to his bedside, as well as those of his children who remained at home. The time had come.

With the others was a young Indian named John Norton. Brant had adopted him and called him his nephew, though they were not blood relations. Norton would carry on Brant's work of translating the New Testament. He had been at work for some time on the Gospel of St. John.

To all those gathered around him just before he died—but especially to Norton—Brant spoke final words that summed up the entire meaning and purpose of his life:

"Have pity on the poor Indians. If you can get any influence with the great, endeavor to do them all the good you can."

Bibliography

BRITT, ALBERT. *Great Indian Chiefs*. New York: McGraw-Hill, 1938.

CHADWICK, EDWARD M. *People of the Longhouse*. Toronto, Ontario: Church of England Publishing Co., 1897.

CHALMERS, HARVEY, in collaboration with ETHEL MONTURE. *Joseph Brant: Mohawk*. East Lansing: Michigan State University Press, 1955.

HALSEY, FRANCIS WHITING. *The Old New York Frontier*. New York: Scribners, 1901.

NORTON, A. TIFFANY. *History of Sullivan's Campaign Against the Iroquois*. Lima, New York: Published by the author, 1879.

STONE, WILLIAM L. *Life of Joseph Brant*. 2 vols. New York: G. Dearborn & Co., 1838. (The standard reference on Brant's life. Nearly every book about Brant written in the last hundred years draws a great deal of its material from this one source.)

VAN EVERY, DALE. *A Company of Heroes*. New York: William Morrow, 1962.

WISSLER, CLARK. *Indians of the United States*. New York: Doubleday, Doran & Co., 1940.

Index